# Southeast Foraging for Beginners

*A Practical Field Guide to Identifying and Harvesting Wild Edibles*

# Table of Contents

# Introduction

Some people forage as a hobby, while others forage because foraged plants are packed with nutrients, antioxidants, and minerals. Many do it because it's a great way to stay active and spend time in nature, and a few forage because their living conditions require them to do so. Even if you don't have a passion or a current need for foraging, you can benefit from learning about this skill. It's crucial for survival and can make the difference between life and death in life-threatening situations. Regardless of why you wish to know about foraging, this book is a beginner's go-to guide to foraging wild edibles and medicinal plants in the Southeast region of the United States.

While learning to forage, you gain other skills and knowledge. Foraging encourages you to immerse yourself in nature, appreciate the beauty around you, and learn about local ecosystems. It teaches you to be mindful, helps you become present in the moment, and reminds you that you're a part of something bigger. This book is easy to understand and follow, ensuring a fruitful learning experience for beginners and more seasoned foragers. Reading it, you'll find detailed information about a wide range of wild edible and medicinal plants in the Southeast and learn to safely and ethically forage them.

Several identification tips and warnings will help you recognize the difference between edible and poisonous plants. You'll find equipment and tool recommendations to safely and efficiently navigate this activity. The book offers information about seasonal foraging, including the unique foraging experience, tips and precautions, and plants you might find in each season. There's an entire chapter dedicated to the fungi and mushrooms of the Southeast. In this chapter, you'll learn the ecological importance of fungi and basic mushroom terminology and anatomy. You'll explore the potential dangers of consuming wild mushrooms and learn to differentiate between edible, inedible, and poisonous species.

This guide delves into the culinary aspect of foraging. You'll find delicious recipes for cooking foraged greens, flowers, berries, roots, and mushrooms and learn helpful cooking tips. You'll learn methods for safely preparing and administering medicinal plants, discover the possibility of harnessing their healing powers, and understand how to incorporate them into your daily life and holistic wellness routine.

In the final chapter, you'll learn to cultivate a forager's mindset and adopt this lifestyle. So, read on and become adept with your new-found love for foraging.

# Chapter 1: Foraging in the Southeast: Getting Started

Known for its mild weather, expansive coastlines, fertile river valleys, lush forests, and closeness to the equator, the rich ecosystems of the Southeast promise a plentiful foraging bounty. As you start your exploration of this region, this chapter brings you profound insight into the practice's history, advice on how to begin, and glimpses into the natural resources awaiting eager foragers.

## The Historical Significance of Foraging

Since the beginning of time, people have enjoyed the benefits of natural resources.[1]

Since the beginning of time, people have enjoyed the benefits of natural resources. Ancient ancestors lived in hunter-gatherer societies, depending on the food they found in their environment. Even after farming and organized agriculture became widespread practices, people continued to rely on foraging and hunting to supplement the nutrients they couldn't get from farming and plant cultivation. They foraged and stored plants that would provide vitamins and nutrients during the months when the weather was poor.

Long after giving up the nomadic lifestyle and moving around to find resources, people continued to rely on occasional foraging and hunting—albeit the practice saw a sharp decline about 500 years ago. After the Industrial Revolution, food production became a regulated economic process, along with gathering and hunting. Amid these regulations, allocated fields for gardens, the rise of supermarkets, and, recently, food delivery services, the ancient practice that shaped civilizations has seemingly vanished.

It was transformed into an urban practice, to be more precise – a leisurely activity reserved for botanists and other nature enthusiasts. In the 19th century, people living in the city enjoyed gathering plants. However, this activity was limited since the most natural areas were off-limits for foraging.

Yet, the appeal of foraging continues to live on. People kept collecting mushrooms, and those living outside the cities continued supplementing their diets with wild edibles. Plants have a wide range of medicinal and ceremonial uses in Indigenous cultures. These communities continue to be shaped by their foraging practices, which are still highly prevalent despite the spread of pastoralism, horticulture, and agriculture. Besides medicine and ceremonies, they rely on gathering wild species to supplement their food sources.

Throughout the 20th century, there have been several revival waves for foraging. For example, the 1960s hippie movement emphasized the importance of reconnecting with nature by encouraging people to engage in wild edible collections as a social engagement. Heavily impacted by the recession, people shared tips and tricks and easily accessible locations so everyone who couldn't afford to buy nutritious produce could supplement their diets. This new attitude toward consumption reflected the beneficial effect of this natural practice on communities. Some set up gardens and orchards on their properties, full of wild edibles and forgotten species ready to be rediscovered (many of these sites exist today). Besides providing support for those in need, people helped others find fulfillment in finding edibles they could use to sustain their families.

Slowly but surely, foraging, once considered a niche activity, has become highly popular again — and it's easy to see why. Besides the widely available channels through which experts can share tips for finding edibles and encouraging them to try new recipes, people have become aware of the many benefits foraging offers for themselves and their environment. People can reduce the impact of invasive species, help the native ones spread, and help the ecosystem thrive through foraging. Moreover, they can source sustainable produce for free. By supporting and learning from local foragers, you can contribute to their efforts to restore your area's ecological health and build a stronger bond with nature.

While picking medicinal plants and deliciously looking berries continues to be popular, people are realizing that foraging has the potential to substitute costly large-scale food production systems. Did you know many people don't know where their food comes from? It applies not only to organic produce but also to everyday plant- and animal-based products. This passive consumption threatens to divide people from the interconnectedness with their natural environment and the intricate systems sustaining them. While foraging has not played a key role in people's diets for over a century, knowing how much can be lost due to this disconnection has made more and more people turn toward learning about this ancient practice.

Beyond the exorbitant costs, food production often comes with consequences, like soil degradation, deforestation, and water pollution. Due to the easy access to information, modern societies are learning how much mindless consumption affects their ecosystems. Moreover, the lack of variety on their plates impacts people's health. Many modern-day chronic diseases are linked to the lack of vitamin-rich food and a preference for highly processed meals, putting enormous pressure on the healthcare system, not to mention on those who can't afford to buy synthetic medicine. Spending time away from nature can negatively affect people's health. Learning how beneficial it is to spend time in a natural environment can make people appreciate its presence and the gifts it offers.

For these reasons, education about the benefits of foraging has never been more popular. People are banding together once again, showing others how to become active participants in the natural food system. You aren't just gathering food when you forage. Moreover, you are not a passive consumer. You're engaging in creating a world of sustainable practices that will benefit you and future generations.

Today's foragers emphasize the importance of becoming attuned to the natural cycles around you. For example, the seasons offer diverse edible groups, catering more fully to your body's needs. Those delicious berries you gather during the fall and winter aren't just tasty additions to your diet. They're full of vitamins, helping you remain healthy during winter.

By taking advantage of what nature offers, you can steer away from consuming processed food. It's opening the gate to a whole new world. A new mindset that lets you see how nature nurtures you and how you can nourish it in return.

In a world of rapid technological development and highly addictive digital gadgets and content, foraging provides another much-needed benefit — spending time in the fresh air and away from technology. Being surrounded by greenery reduces the stress of a fast-paced lifestyle. It can help people cope with depression and anxiety and boost mood. Foraging involves a lot of walking around, which is another benefit for people's well-being. It's a low-impact activity many enjoy merely to move their bodies, and finding wild edibles is a bonus. Still, the satisfaction of finding foraged goods offers a wonderful experience. Knowing they're successful in doing something good not only for themselves but for their environment can improve a forager's self-esteem.

Traditional foragers in Indigenous and other rural communities have developed a massive body of knowledge, allowing them to sustain their cultural traditions and spiritual practices. Many rely on a profound understanding and appreciation of nature and its gifts. For them, foraging is as much about giving back as it is about gaining sustenance. For modern societies, learning from these foragers can promote the spreading of ecological knowledge, awareness of ancient traditions, and cultural diversity while addressing cultural appropriation issues.

Beginners and those only considering dipping their toes into foraging often question its sustainability. Among all the knowledge available to people, there is plenty of misinformation. For example, many proclaim that foraging can negatively affect biodiversity. Quite the contrary, it has the power to safeguard endangered species by eliminating invasive intruders, which could lead to them becoming endangered.

In urban areas, foraging for invasive species can generate a massive cultural and socioeconomic for communities supplementing their diets with wild edibles. By targeting threats to local ecosystems, you can help your community benefit from the resources nature provides. You're supporting the conservation and growth of the native flora, leaving more for others to find. For the same reason, modern foraging practices are centered on learning the conservation status of local species before gathering them. Moreover, they emphasize paying attention to individual plants and small plant groups, which may suffer the consequences of overharvesting. By letting these thrive, you can enrich the biodiversity that will be available in the future.

Another benefit modern societies are discovering in foraging is community building. When you collect food, you're building relationships with your community. People rarely forage alone, not because it's not recommended for safety reasons. It's a fun activity that brings people together. As you learn and reach out for information about the species in your area, you'll see how strong foraging communities can be. You'll become part of this fantastic community, which will help you in more ways than merely avoiding the risks of picking toxic plants and mushrooms.

Moreover, by involving others, you spread the joy of foraging. By creating a group, you let the camaraderie and collective sense of satisfaction make it stronger. Foraging communities care for their members for safety reasons and to empower them with the knowledge to make their ecosystems healthier and more prosperous.

In the 21st century, foraging has gained an entirely new layer to its historical significance. In an age of biodiversity loss, when people are truly experiencing the devastating effects of climate change, doing more to help than to destroy has become a number one goal for many. They understand that taking and giving from nature are actions interconnected in an ancient cycle that needs assistance to sustain itself. Due to the massive population growth spike in the past century, people have taken far more than they were giving back. Foraging is a wonderful way to change this problem. More importantly, when considering all the benefits, you don't have to give up taking to give back either. You gain more by helping the native ecosystems thrive than by being a passive consumer. You're gaining food rich in nutrients, new flavors to spruce up your dishes, a learning experience, and a broader perspective of how the planet works. You'll find a stark reminder that you're part of the ecosystem, breaking down the inherent barriers between you and the natural world around you. Whether this practice is entirely new to you or you have heard of it before but haven't had the chance to try it, what it teaches will significantly shape your future — as it did for the generations who engaged in foraging throughout history.

# The Enchanting Nature of the Southeast

The Southeast has abundant natural resources, and the war lands offer everything from minerals to plants to water. Coupled with the region's warm and sunny climate, these enhancing natural resources attracted people to settle and make a living in the Southeast. Beyond the crops that feed the animals, the Southeastern states also potentially provide a bountiful harvest of wild edibles.

For example, the Southeast boasts unique species of wild greens, which thrive in the mild spring weather prevailing in the region. While spring often turns into summer very quickly, the number of wild greens you can harvest in this short window is highly significant.

# Practical Tips for Novices

As beneficial foraging as is, the stakes are high. However, with the proper precautions, you can avoid putting yourself or anyone else in danger. When embarking on your Southeast foraging journey, keeping a few safety tips in mind is crucial.

### Exercise Caution

Learn how to identify the plants before reaching for them in the fields. If possible, explore the territory with a foraging expert's help. If not, acquire multiple guidebooks specific to your region and research online databases so you can cross-reference your findings. You may even benefit from taking a foraging course.

Learning to recognize toxic plants isn't about avoiding a nasty rash or unpleasant food poisoning. Some can cause serious health issues and even death.

Allergies are another factor to consider. If you haven't eaten a wild plant or fungi before, you can't know if you're allergic to it. Consume your wild edibles in small portions to be safe. If no reactions arise, you can increase the quantities. If you have unusual symptoms, like a rash, itching, difficulty breathing, nausea, etc., seek medical help as soon as possible.

Before touching a plant or fungi, use your senses. If it looks too bright and has a strong odor, it may cause suspicion. Does it look or smell precisely like the guidebook says it should? Or does it have some dissimilarities? Your senses will sharpen with practice, but until they do, relying on trusted guides is best.

Allergies are another factor to consider when foraging.[1]

Wear clean clothes during harvesting and use clean tools (clean them before foraging adventures). This helps avoid transferring disease or seeds of invasive plants into different areas.

Be aware of how plants and fungi should be prepared. Some wild edibles can only be consumed after cooking, while others require only a wash before eating.

Never use plastic containers for harvesting. Water continues to evaporate from harvested plants and plant parts. If it's trapped in a plastic container, it can lead to the formation of mildew. Mildewed plants are unsafe for consumption, so it's best to avoid this by collecting everything in breathable bags or containers.

### Understanding the Region

Look up the most common edible species in the area you plan to forage. Are there dangerous lookalikes nearby? If so, how can you avoid confusing them? Learn what endangered and invasive species are in the region so that you know which to leave alone and which to forage.

Also, it's highly recommended to study the areas where water and soil may be contaminated (for example, roads, golf courses, factories, etc.). You should avoid these areas and stick to the areas away from heavy human activity.

### Focus on Weeds

Like in any region, the Southeast has an abundance of weeds. Since they grow more aggressively, you won't deplete them by foraging. Look for patches where lots of edible weeds grow when foraging and have your fill.

### Forage Only Healthy Plants

It may seem apparent, but plants that don't appear to be their typical, healthy selves shouldn't be consumed. It varies from plant to plant. Therefore, before foraging, always know what a healthy-looking plant looks like and talk about it with your foraging mentor or expert.

### Only Take What You Need

Edibles are best used fresh or within a short period (except those used in dried form). If you don't plan to preserve your findings, only take what you can use in the next few days. Leave the rest behind. You can pick them (and maybe even more) during your next adventure.

### Start with What You're Comfortable with

Foraging varies based on native and non-native species in the area, season, geography, etc. Stick to the species you're comfortable identifying when learning the ropes. Learning what species are poisonous can help you avoid them and only pick what you know is undoubtedly edible.

### Leave No Trace

When you venture off trails, you risk damaging the region's flora. Avoid this by sticking to well-traveled paths or only walking on rocks and logs without trampling the plants as you go.

Never litter during foraging adventures. Pack up any trash you've created while consuming snacks, drinks, etc. Picking up anything left behind by others (as it could endanger the animals and the plants) is also recommended. If you forage with others, hold them accountable and remind them to be mindful of their impact on nature.

## Be Mindful of the Weather

Foraging is an outdoor activity, so staying up to date with the weather forecast when you're heading out is advisable.[a]

Foraging is an outdoor activity, so staying up to date with the weather forecast when you're heading out is advisable. It will help you appropriately prepare for foraging and emergencies and maximize your productivity.

### Ethical Considerations

Foragers benefit from forging a connection with the natural world — but they also have a responsibility to respect it and preserve the precarious balance of its ecosystems. Foraging sustainably and ethically, especially as the popularity of this practice soars, is crucial.

### Be Responsible

Learn about the sensitive habitats in the area and stay away from them – until you understand how to forage mindfully. There must be enough for regrowth and to sustain the wildlife.

You may be eager to find many goods in your foraging adventures, but be prepared for this won't always be the case. Sometimes, you'll return home without a massive yield — but all the richer for the experiences you've gained about your environment. When learning the ropes, simply enjoying the outdoors and learning about the region and its ecosystem will be far more valuable than a bag full of edibles. Even later, your bounty may vary depending on the weather, animal activity, and other outside factors.

If you only find a small patch, leave it to grow. It will reward you (and other foragers) with plenty of gifts later. Only take from larger patches and, even then, practice moderation. Leave some for others, and let the area regrow naturally.

If you aren't taking entire plants, make sure you cut the leaves and other plants with a clean, sharp tool to avoid damaging the plant. In this way, the plants can grow and thrive and provide you and other foragers with plenty of natural resources in the future.

If you're unsure whether the region you plan to forage is sensitive or not, look up harvesting limitations that may apply or local land management guidelines. As a rule of thumb, you shouldn't take more than five percent of one species from one spot, but in sensitive habitats, your consumption may be more limited (or completely off-limits).

### Learn the Best Way to Harvest Each Species

Understanding the optimal method for harvesting plants is one of the finest methods to guarantee that the ones you leave behind may thrive for a long time. Different edibles require diverse practices for harvesting sustainably. For example, some plants can only be cut, others should be pulled up with the roots, and a third group may require a specific way of removing its parts, etc. When you research the local forage goods, learn how to harvest them.

### Don't Share Your Location

While geotagging foraging locations can be helpful for beginners, you don't want to share these online with everyone. It can lead to overcrowding and depletion of edibles, not to mention overall natural resource degradation (as plants are fundamental parts of the resource ecosystem).

### Enjoy Your Connection with Nature

Foraging is much more than an enjoyable pastime. It's a way to contribute to the environment and your health. It's a way to cultivate a deep connection and familiarity with the natural world. When you forage, you're embarking on a learning journey of taking advantage of what nature has given you, advocating for vulnerable resources, and finding the balance between what you need for food and medicine and giving back enough for sustainable cohabitation. This book will guide you on this path of exploration of the diverse, delicious, and sustainable world of wild edibles waiting to be discovered in the Southeast. Take the opportunity to enjoy your budding connection with nature.

# Chapter 2: Foraging Equipment, Tools, and Safety

Now that you've seen the allure of foraging in the Southeast, it's time to shift your focus toward the preparation. This chapter enlists the safety precautions, common foraging tools and their care, and additional helpful equipment to help you approach this activity with increased awareness of its hazards and how to shield yourself from them.

## Preparation

As with any outdoor activity, you must be prepared when foraging. Gone are the times when people were accustomed to the perils of inclement weather, rough terrain, and encounters with potentially dangerous animals. Living in an urban environment (even if you live near a natural area and not in a big city), you are not likely to spend hours walking on varied terrains. The Southeastern region features mountainous areas in the Appalachians, expansive river valleys like the Mississippi Delta, and coastal plains along the Gulf of Mexico and the Atlantic Ocean. You must study the exact setting you're about to forage to avoid exposure to potentially life-threatening situations. Besides researching the terrain, you should also research the equipment you need. For example, you'll likely need different footwear and clothes when foraging in rough, rocky mountain terrain than near the rivers.

The Southeast region's climate ranges from humid subtropical in the coastal plains to humid continental in the mountainous areas. Hurricanes, flash floods, and tropical storms can occur almost without warning from spring through summer. Still, by following the weather forecast, you'll be better prepared for your adventure. For example, when the weather is warming up, you'll know to bring more water and adequate sun protection. Have a plan on what to do in the worst-case scenario with unpredictable weather changes. Where do you go if you are surprised by a tropical storm? Learn how to seek shelter (quickly) in case of flash floods. Besides these, there could be other common weather occurrences in your region (for example, wildfires have also become increasingly frequent in the Southeast), so look them up alongside ways to prepare for them.

Another reason to keep up to date with the weather forecast is knowing what's in season for foraging. You'll be more successful in gathering a variety of edibles by being mindful of the season. For example, spring is excellent for wild greens, summer for berries, and fall for nuts, while winter is excellent for foraging cold-resistant varieties.

### Understand What You're Looking for

Now that you know what's in season, learn everything you can about the goods you're looking for. Are they widely available in your area? Where is their natural habitat? Are there toxic species that look like edible ones? Identifying the species you want to forage beforehand lowers the chances of confusing them with unwanted ones, not to mention sparing yourself the time and effort of looking for something in the wrong place.

Another perk of preparing to harvest specific species is knowing what to take. You'll know how much you can take without damaging the plants or their ecosystem.

### Avoid Foraging Alone

Whenever possible, forage in groups. Remember, safety in numbers is essential, so if something happens to anyone, others can help. Even if you can only find one person (for beginners, going with an experienced foraging mentor is highly recommended), it's better than going alone. The more sets of eyes you have, the safer you'll be.

# Essential Foraging Tools

Below is a compilation of essential foraging tools and how they help make foraging easier and safer.

### Pruners

Pruners are an essential tool for harvesting and processing plants.'

Pruners are an essential tool for harvesting and processing plants. They are especially handy for cutting roots, small branches, twigs, and herbaceous stems. If foraging for these regularly, keeping your pruners in a holster or a portion of your bag where you can easily reach them is highly recommended.

Invest in a high-quality pair that can be properly sharpened and cleaned. Poor quality ones can rust and dull quickly, and neither is conducive for safe foraging. Dull blades can damage plants, so you could destroy the entire specimen even if you only plan to take a small part.

Another tip: Look for pruners designed to reduce hand strain. Try them in the store to see how they fit in your hands. They shouldn't exceed the width of your extended grasp when fully open.

## Shovel

Grab a strong shovel that can handle the workload of foraging in heavily compacted soil.*

This may be a tool you already have, but it's worth investing in several foraging types. For example, for large-rooted plants, you need a long-handled shovel with a pointed blade (it needs to dig into the ground so it can't be flat). Grab a strong shovel that can handle the workload of foraging in heavily compacted soil.

## Kitchen Scissors

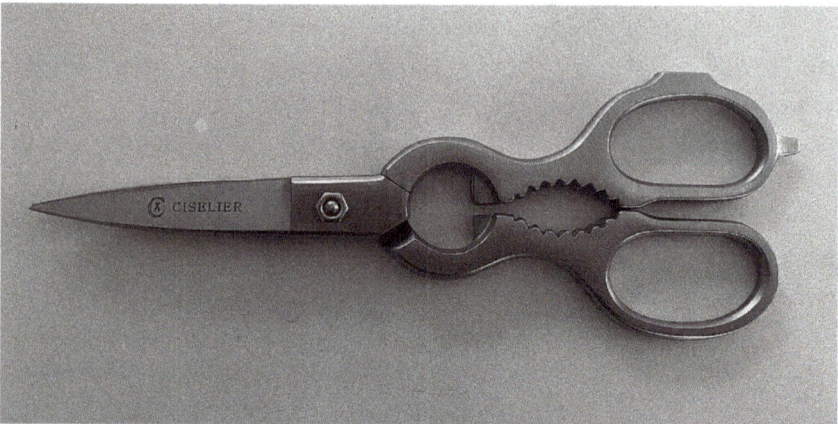

Another must-have for your foraging adventures is kitchen scissors.*

Another must-have for your foraging adventures is kitchen scissors. Unlike pruners, they are more suitable for harvesting tender species. They have a longer-reaching blade and won't damage the plants when cutting stems, leaves, flowers, etc. You must keep them clean between foraging, so having a separate, high-quality pair only for foraging is advisable.

### Digging Fork

Digging forks are great for loosening the soil and lifting the branching rootage free from the ground.[7]

When gathering small, tender roots and soil that is not too compact, digging forks will be the right tools for the job. They're great for loosening the soil and lifting the branching rootage free from the ground. If you're going for whole plants, start with the digging fork, especially in densely populated vegetation.

The fork's sturdy and square lines will easily enter the earth, but they won't cut into the roots because they're not bendable. Using them will make it less likely to damage roots and disturb the vegetation around them. Still, it may take some trial and error until you learn how to use them safely (practice on non-edible and non-poisonous weeds before you dig up edibles). As always, go for a higher quality option for a reliable tool in the long run.

## Weeding or Japanese Garden Knife

Try a weeding knife if foraging in more stubborn, compact soil and are worried about damaging the roots.*

Try a weeding knife if foraging in more stubborn, compact soil and are worried about damaging the roots. These sturdy tools can break the ground, pry small rocks out of the way, and free small-to-mid-sized rootage without cutting into it. Moreover, you can use them for dividing roots— they're safe.

Instead of plastic, choose sturdier wooden-handled knives that last longer. Some have a protective piece at the base of the blade to prevent cutting yourself in case your hand slips.

## Pruning Saw

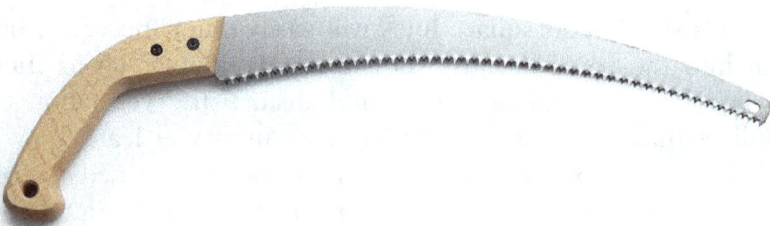

Invest in a foldable pruning saw if you are foraging small to mid-sized branches and tree limbs (for medicinal purposes).*

Invest in a foldable pruning saw if you are foraging small to mid-sized branches and tree limbs (for medicinal purposes). They're the only way to harvest these safely and avoid damaging the trees you're removing them from.

### Knives

A sturdy, compact folding knife will come in handy when foraging bark. Get one with a sheath to make carrying easier. On the other hand, if you're cutting up tough roots on the terrain (it's sometimes easier to transport them if they're not in one large piece), you'll need a heavy-duty chopping knife. As always, invest in rust-resistant and quality tools that won't damage the plants or endanger your safety.

### Vegetable Brush with Bristles

These are excellent for cleaning roots from the soil, small rocks, and perhaps small animals from the roots.[10]

These are excellent for cleaning roots from the soil, small rocks, and perhaps small animals from the roots. You can scrub them clean in no time. However, avoid being too rough, especially with tender roots, as the bristles can harm or break them.

## Holster

While a holster is optional (you can shove everything into your bag), it makes using the tools much more manageable.[11]

As you've seen from the items listed above, there are plenty of tools you want to keep at hand. While a holster is optional (you can shove everything into your bag), it makes using the tools much more manageable. You can keep them organized in a multi-space hip holster and take them out when needed. After cleaning them, you can put them back and have them ready for their next job.

## Field Guide

A field guide should have information on the plants and fungi's medical and nutritious properties, along with clear photographs and detailed descriptions for easier identification.[13]

Lastly, always take your field guide with you. As much as you study the intended forages, their habitat, and lookalikes, in nature, looks can be deceiving. You want a frame of reference with you on the terrain. When in doubt, always look up if it's the species you're looking for (or think you've found). Ensure the guide is tailored to the specific area and is the most updated version. It should have information on the plants and fungi's medical and nutritious properties, along with clear photographs and detailed descriptions for easier identification.

# Safety

Safety is a top priority when foraging in the wild. It requires a risk-aware mindset to cultivate by following the tips below.

### Be Aware of Your Surroundings

It's easy to lose your sense of direction when on unfamiliar terrain. Besides educating yourself about the area layout, you must activate your senses when heading out to forage. Look where you're going and avoid stepping into areas that look unsafe. Likewise, be on the lookout for animal encounters. You may encroach on their territory, making them act defensively, even if they're usually friendly.

Another tip: know if the area is public or private property. Avoid foraging on privately owned land. You must have the owner's permission if you do.

### Handling Snakes and Other Venomous Animals

Venomous animals, like wasps and snakes, inject toxins into the bloodstream through a sting or bite. While some venomous snakes are easy to distinguish, it's best to avoid disturbing them all if you're unfamiliar with the slithering creatures. Give them space if you see one and are unsure if it's venomous. In most cases, they'll go away because they won't see you as a threat, unlike if you make threatening moves toward them. Suppose you venture into an area where snakes are common. In that case, it's recommended to wear adequate protection, including sturdy boots, snake gaiters that go above the knee, and long pants.

### Bugs and Spiders

Most venomous spiders are reclusive, but it's best to stay clear of their territory as they might bite if provoked and threatened. Spiders are predators, so they hang around where there is prey (typically flies), like under piles of leaves, rocks, and other debris.

If you're bitten by a spider or bug (even a non-venomous one), the area will likely swell. This is normal. Depending on the swelling, you may have to remove part of a garment constricting the area and wash the skin.

### Bees, Wasps, and Hornets

These insects are common during the warmer months, building hives or nests under roof edges, in the trees, on the ground, or in rarely-used equipment and machinery. In dry weather, they might be attracted to food and drinks as they seek moisture to remain hydrated. Keep food and drink you bring to foraging in containers to avoid inviting them and exposing yourself to potential attacks.

The most significant concern with bee or wasp stings is an allergic reaction. Never go foraging without an epinephrine auto-injector if you have a history of sting-related allergic reactions. Still, stings can be painful (especially wasps and hornets), even if you aren't allergic. Try to scrape the stinger out of your skin as soon as you're bitten, as this will remove some toxins.

### Fire Ants

The sting of the fire ants can also be toxic, and unfortunately, the chances are, you won't be stung by only one. Unknowingly, you can step into the middle of their underground nests, and within seconds, you'll be under an attack from the entire colony. If this happens, use a piece of cloth or your hands to wipe the ants off you and your clothes.

Besides being painful, fire ant stings can develop into blister-like sores and become infected, so you must keep the area clean following the incident.

### Preventing Bug Bites and Stings

Some insects are also disease carriers, so avoiding their bites and stings while foraging is crucial.

Here are a few additional tips to prevent bug bites and stings:

- **Use Insect Repellent:** This is a must for all foragers. There are products with different strengths based on how much time you spend outdoors. For longer foraging adventures, pick a stronger one.

- **Avoid Well-Known Breeding Grounds:** Some insects love to breed in areas near water (like mosquitos), while others prefer different territories. Stay away from these areas, especially when the insects are the most active.

- **Keep Yourself Covered:** Wear clothes that cover most of your body when venturing into wooded and high grass areas. For instance, long-sleeved shirts tucked in long pants, and boots or footwear you can tuck your pants into. This may be a struggle on warmer days, but you can wear breathable fabrics that provide adequate protection without making you uncomfortable.

- **Check for Ticks:** Clothing may provide coverage for some insects, but ticks can attack your hair, shoes, clothes, and accessories and travel to hard-to-reach places on your body (i.e., the neck, behind the knee, groin, armpit, and scalp). If you spend time in wooded or high grass areas, always check for ticks upon returning home. If you're confident in removing them, grab them with fine-tipped tweezers close to the skin and lift them off with upward pressure.

### When to Call for Help

When you're bitten by a snake or encounter a poisonous plant, insect, or other animal and experience a severe reaction (like difficulty breathing), alert those around you (another reason never to forage alone). If you're alone, call emergency services. If you're bitten or think you've been poisoned by a plant but are not experiencing symptoms and are unsure what to do next, contact your local poison control center.

# Clothing, Footwear and Additional Equipment

The clothes worn while foraging can be a game-changer. Sturdy, waterproof shoes (often foraging includes venturing into wet areas), warm layers, a good rain jacket, protective pants, and suitable gloves are essential. Depending on where and what you forage, you'll need protection from thorns, vines, and stinging plants or animals. Keep a rain jacket in your bag, too, even if there is no chance of rain (you never know in the Southeast). Always keep the area's outlay in mind and wear terrain-appropriate shoes at all times.

### Gloves

Foraging can be demanding on the skin, and your hands will thank you for investing in quality gloves.[18]

Foraging can be demanding on the skin, and your hands will thank you for investing in quality gloves. Look for durable, double-lined, comfortable gloves to prevent blistering. Having two pairs in your bag might be a good idea—a thinner pair for handling dainty plant parts and a thicker pair for handling prickly or rough materials.

# Hand Lens or Other Magnifying Tool

Invest in a hand lens, preferably one with 10 to 20 times magnification.[14]

Invest in a hand lens, preferably one with 10 to 20 times magnification. It will help you identify plants that can only be distinguished through tiny parts. Even better, get one with an LED lamp attached, and you'll have the perfect lighting for proper plant or mushroom identification.

## A Sturdy Backpack

To carry all of your foraging supplies, including food, drink, and any necessary tools (including sun protection and a first aid kit), you'll need a sturdy backpack.[15]

To carry all of your foraging supplies, including food, drink, and any necessary tools (including sun protection and a first aid kit), you'll need a sturdy backpack. Get a backpack that will fit comfortably over your shoulders and have lots of compartments to keep your goods organized.

## Containers

It's often a matter of preference when choosing portable storage containers.[16]

It's often a matter of preference when choosing portable storage containers. Consider what you would be comfortable carrying around for hours. It shouldn't be something heavy or too fragile that you must be careful about when carrying. Still, you should consider how much and what material you want to place your collected foods in. If you aim for larger amounts, carrying them in a small container won't work because everything will get squashed. Likewise, if you plan to forage something with an unusual shape, account for this when choosing the container.

Also, consider how you'll place your edibles into the containers. Do you plan to wrap damp clothes around them to keep them from wilting? Mesh bags work well for shielding and separating plant material. Think about what will work depending on what you harvest, how you plan to use it, and how long it will take you to take it home.

## Baskets

Wood baskets are perfect for harvesting medicinal herbs.[17]

Wood baskets are perfect for harvesting medicinal herbs, especially if you only need a small amount, as you can leave them inside to dry. Look for those with a looser, open weave for better ventilation.

## 5-Gallon Buckets

If you're harvesting muddy rooted plants, keeping them in 5-gallon buckets will be an excellent way to retain their freshness.[18]

If you're harvesting muddy rooted plants, keeping them in 5-gallon buckets will be an excellent way to retain their freshness. The same applies to large-scale forages when you want to keep the plant's roots in water to prevent wilting. However, this may be too bulky to carry, so it will only work on short-distance trips.

## A Reliable Method of Communication

Contacting people or emergency services is paramount when you're in the wilderness. A fully charged phone and solar chargers are a must. You may want to invest in other radio-frequency-operated communication devices in case you don't have cell phone or internet coverage.

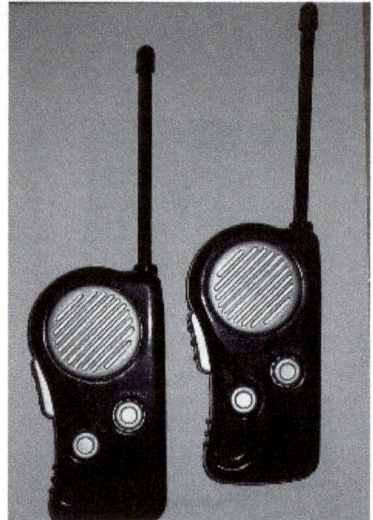

You may want to invest in other radio-frequency-operated communication devices in case you don't have cell phone or internet coverage.[19]

## A Compass and Map

A compass and map are indispensable tools for navigating the great outdoors. Look for an easy-to-read but detailed map of the terrain, including topographical information. Likewise, your compass should be straightforward and have a compact, durable housing.

A compass and map are indispensable tools for navigating the great outdoors.[20]

## A First Aid Kit

A first aid kit is a must-have for foraging. Always have a kit with all the necessary medical supplies (bandages, pain relievers, antiseptic, tweezers, etc.) in your bag.

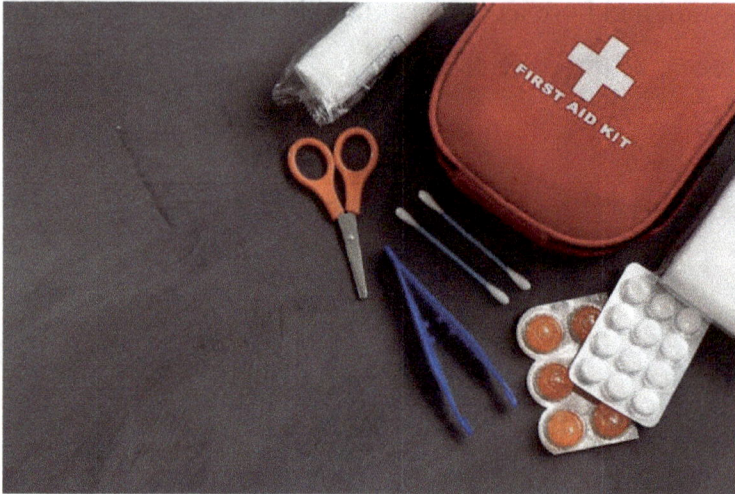

A first aid kit is a must-have for foraging.[31]

## Water Bottle and Snacks

Proper hydration and nourishment are fundamental for staying safe outdoors. Bring plenty of water and snacks, like energy bars and nuts, to keep you energized and focused on your foraging adventure.

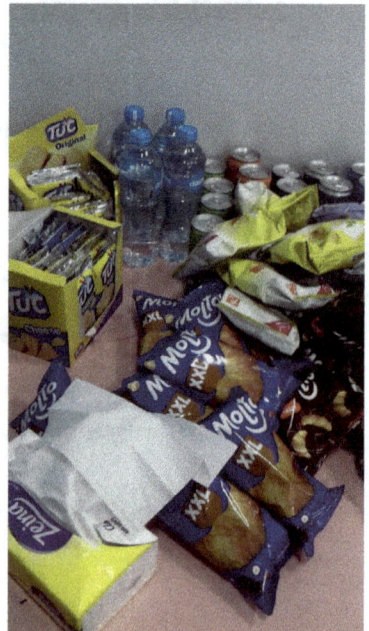

Proper hydration and nourishment are fundamental for staying safe outdoors.[32]

# Maintaining and Caring for Tools

High-quality tools will last for years, but only if you regularly care for and maintain them. To ensure they will be ready to serve you on your next foraging adventure, follow the basic maintenance rules described below:

Remove the soil and debris from your digging tools after each use. Investing in proper housing for them (or buying them with it) will make this easier. If you can slide them in and out, it will remove the dirt. If you can't, or if your tools don't have proper housing, use a sharp tool like a screwdriver to scrape off the debris.

Naturally, this implies that the tools are dry when you put them away. Letting them dry is imperative; otherwise, they could rust and rot. If you're not using them for a more extended period (or want to add extra protection), coat the wooden handles with linseed oil. Wipe the metal parts of your tools clean with a cloth and spray them lightly with an oil made for this purpose. Sharpen the shovels, knives, and the digging and cutting tools regularly with a stone or whetstone. If the digging tools and shovels developed ragged edges, file them smooth.

# A Final Word

Safety preparation is as paramount for a successful and fulfilling foraging experience as it is for getting the proper tools and equipment. A well-prepared forager is observant and considers the well-being of themselves and the environment. You can venture into foraging adventures confident that you'll keep yourself and your environment safe by raising your awareness of your surroundings.

# Chapter 3: Seasonal Foraging in the Southeast

There is nothing more seasonal than wild edible plants. Imagine biting into a wild strawberry, its sweet juice bursting in your mouth, but knowing that these little red gems are only around for about two weeks. On the other hand, Loomis's mountain mint can be gathered all summer. Its refreshing aroma is a constant companion during the warmer months. This guide will help you understand what is in season, when, and where in the Southeast so you can make the most of nature's changing bounty.

Weather is crucial when foraging, especially in the Southeast, where it can vary significantly from year to year and state to state. With its lingering chill and sporadic snow flurries, March weather in Kentucky is vastly different from the mild, early spring temperatures of Alabama. This variability means the same plant could be ready for harvest at various times, depending on where you are. Hence, being in tune with local weather patterns is essential for successful foraging.

For example, in early spring, you might be eagerly searching for ramps (wild leeks) on the damp, shaded forest floors of North Carolina. Their intense, garlicky aroma and flavor are a delight, but timing is everything— they're only available for a few short weeks. In contrast, the forests and fields of Georgia come alive with blackberries and blueberries as summer unfolds. The sun-soaked days are perfect for picking these juicy berries, which can be eaten fresh, baked into pies, or preserved as jams to savor long after the season has passed.

The lists in this seasonal guide include specific plant parts when necessary. For instance, you might see "daylily shoots" mentioned because this part of the plant is exceptionally tender and flavorful. At other times, a plant's name may be listed without specifying a part, indicating that the entire plant is edible. You'll find detailed profiles for each plant explaining how to collect, prepare, and eat different parts. This information ensures you can safely and effectively enjoy the bounty of wild edibles.

Picture a crisp fall day in the Southeast, where the air is filled with the earthy scent of fallen leaves and the crunch of hickory nuts underfoot. Foragers can delight in the abundance of nuts, such as pecans and chestnuts, perfect for roasting or adding to baked goods. Fall is prime time for wild grapes and persimmons, their rich flavors offering a sweet treat as the weather cools. Also, don't forget the thrill of finding chanterelles and hen-of-the-woods mushrooms after a refreshing rain.

Winter foraging in the Southeast is a unique experience. While the landscape may seem barren, hardy greens like chickweed and wild mustard continue to thrive, offering fresh, nutritious options even in the coldest months. Imagine the satisfaction of gathering these resilient plants on a brisk winter morning, the frosty air invigorating your senses.

Each season brings challenges and rewards. Spring's abundance can be tempered by the risk of encountering poison ivy or venomous snakes. Summer's heat and humidity demand careful preparation and hydration. Fall's bounty requires vigilance to avoid poisonous look-alikes and awareness of larger wildlife. Winter's limited daylight and cold temperatures necessitate warm clothing and careful planning.

This chapter aims to paint a vivid picture of the ever-changing landscape of foraging in the Southeast. By understanding the seasonal availability of wild edibles and each season's unique conditions, you can deepen your connection to nature and enjoy the diverse flavors each season offers. So, whether you're a seasoned forager or beginning your journey, let this guide be your companion as you explore the rich, dynamic world of seasonal foraging in the Southeast.

# Spring

Spring in the Southeast is a season of transformation, a time when the landscape comes alive with a burst of new growth.[38]

Spring in the Southeast is a season of transformation, a time when the landscape comes alive with a burst of new growth. This season can vary in length and intensity, sometimes arriving quickly with a flurry of activity, while at other times, it unfolds slowly, offering a prolonged period of mild weather and budding plants. Regardless of how it arrives, spring in the Southeast is divided into early and late phases, each with unique offerings.

In early spring, the first signs of life emerge from the ground as perennial leafy plants reach their peak, like wild lettuce. It's the perfect time to look for asparagus-like pokeweed shoots that are tender and full of flavor. The temperatures during this period can be quite variable, with warm days followed by chilly nights affecting the availability and timing of edible plants. For instance, the delicate blossoms of redbud trees can linger for weeks or disappear quickly depending on the weather. This unpredictability means foragers must stay vigilant, ready to seize the opportunity to harvest when conditions are just right.

Imagine walking through an open meadow or along the edges of sunny areas in early spring. You may find yourself amid a wealth of edible plants like dandelion greens, which are tender and slightly bitter, perfect for a fresh salad. Field garlic can add a delightful kick to your dishes with its mild onion flavor. Keep an eye out for the vibrant purple blooms of redbud trees, whose blossoms are not only beautiful but also edible, adding a splash of color to your meals.

As the season progresses to mid and late spring, the landscape continues to change, and new plants come into focus. For example, black locust flowers bloom in clusters, offering a sweet treat enjoyed raw or cooked. In sunny areas, you might find basswood blossoms, which can be used to make a soothing tea. The fragrant flowers of elderberry bushes appear, heralding the approach of summer and providing a source of delicious, nutrient-rich blossoms.

The woodlands and partially shaded places of the Southeast are equally bountiful in spring. Here, you'll find basswood leaves, tender and mild, perfect for adding to salads. Beech leaves are another early spring delicacy, offering a fresh, slightly tangy flavor. If you're lucky, you may stumble upon a patch of ramps, their garlicky scent guiding you to one of the most prized wild edibles of the season.

Wetlands, riverbanks, and lakesides are teeming with life in spring. Cattail shoots, often referred to as "Cossack asparagus," can be harvested for their tender, nutritious cores. With its peppery flavor, the watercress thrives in these damp areas, adding a zesty kick to your springtime meals.

Foragers in coastal areas will find their unique treasures. Glasswort stems and leaves offer a salty crunch, ideal for adding to salads or pickling. Sea rocket, another coastal plant, provides a sharp, mustard-like flavor, enhancing a variety of dishes.

Spring foraging comes with its share of challenges and precautions. The resurgence of plant life means poisonous plants like poison ivy and poison oak are more prevalent. Identifying these harmful plants to avoid unpleasant encounters is essential. Additionally, venomous snakes become more active as the weather warms, so remaining cautious and aware of your surroundings is imperative.

Despite these challenges, spring is a time of abundance and renewal. The early morning hours are often the best time for foraging when the air is still cool and the dew glistens on the leaves. This is when you'll find the plants at their freshest and most vibrant, ready to be gathered and enjoyed. Whether seasoned forager or new to the practice, spring in the Southeast offers a wealth of opportunities to connect with nature and experience the joy of harvesting wild edibles.

# Summer

Summer in the Southeast is synonymous with abundant fruit and vibrant plant life. This season, stretching from early June through August, offers a rich tapestry of wild edibles in various terrains, from open meadows to shaded woodlands and coastal areas. The intense heat and humidity of summer bring bounty and challenges for foragers, making preparation and timing crucial.

Early to midsummer is the prime time for foraging wild fruits. Picture walking along a sunny trail – the air is thick with the sweet scent of ripe blackberries and raspberries. These berries, wineberries, and strawberries provide a delicious and nutritious treat. Imagine plucking a handful of these juicy gems, their sweet-tart flavor bursting in your mouth as you savor the taste of summer.

In addition to the early summer fruit, late summer has unique offerings. Often described as a tropical-tasting fruit native to North America, pawpaw ripens in the shady understories of forests. Muscadine, the wild grape of the South, and maypop, a passion fruit, are also ready for harvest. These fruits can be enjoyed fresh or to make preserves, wines, and desserts, capturing the essence of summer long after the season has ended.

Beyond fruit, summer is a season of thriving leafy greens and other unique plant parts. Lemony wood sorrel adds a refreshing zing to salads, while the menthol-like aroma of Loomis's mountain mint can invigorate your senses. With its earthy flavor, Shiso is perfect for adding depth to summer dishes. You may find sweet oxeye daisy leaves, tangy sumac fruit clusters, and root beer–like sassafras roots ready for gathering.

Imagine foraging in open meadows or along sunny edges. Here, you might encounter the bright blue flowers of Asiatic dayflower, the juicy berries of black cherries, or the sweet clusters of elderberries. Field mustard flowers and seedpods can be harvested to add a spicy note to your meals, while wild strawberries and blueberries offer a sweet snack. Keep an eye out for the unique flowers of kudzu, used to make jellies, and the delicate blooms of honeysuckle, perfect for infusing syrups and teas.

Woodlands and partially shaded places offer a rich variety of edibles. Basswood seeds, black birch twigs, bark, and black nightshade fruit can be found in these cooler, shaded areas. In these spots, you may discover the vibrant flowers of False Solomon's seal or the spicy leaves and twigs of Spicebush. Pawpaw and mayapple fruit ripens in these areas, and their unique flavors are waiting to be enjoyed.

Seashore and coastal areas are not to be overlooked. Beach plum fruit is perfect for making preserves because of its tart flavor. Glasswort stems offer a salty crunch, ideal for salads or pickling. Sea purslane leaves and stems can be harvested for their succulent, slightly salty taste, adding a coastal flair to your foraged meals.

Wetlands, riverbanks, and lakesides provide their own set of treasures. American lotus tubers and seeds, often considered a delicacy, can be harvested with cattail flowers and pollen, adding a unique texture and flavor to dishes. Watercress flowers thrive in these wet environments, offering a fresh, spicy kick to summer salads with their peppery taste.

While summer is a time of abundance, it also brings challenges. The intense heat and humidity can make foraging uncomfortable and potentially hazardous. Staying hydrated and protecting yourself from the sun by wearing hats, sunscreen, and lightweight, breathable clothing is essential. Mosquitoes and other biting insects are at their peak during this time, so using insect repellent and wearing long sleeves and pants helps minimize discomfort.

Despite these challenges, the rewards of summer foraging are plentiful. When the temperatures are cooler, the early mornings and late evenings are the best times to venture out. It's when you can experience the beauty of nature at its peak, with the vibrant colors of wildflowers, the buzzing of bees, and the sweet, ripe fruit waiting to be harvested. Summer in the Southeast offers a rich and diverse foraging experience, inviting you to explore and enjoy the natural bounty of this dynamic season.

# Fall

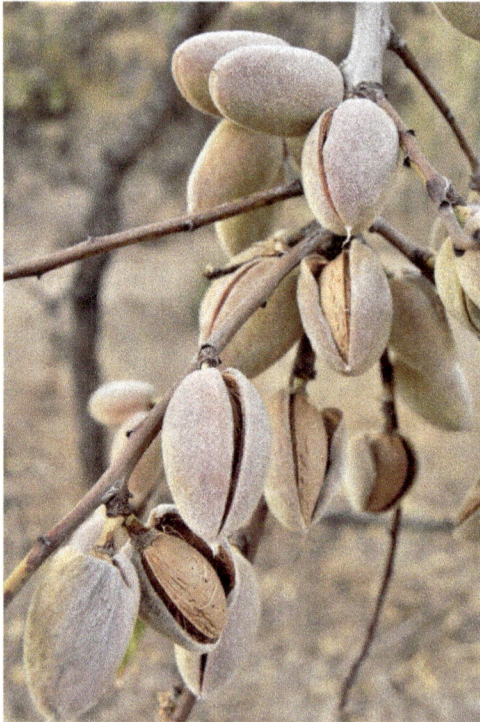

Once fall fully arrives, it brings a rich harvest, especially known for its nuts.[25]

Fall in the Southeast often starts later than in other regions, with weather that fluctuates wildly. Even in early November, you may find some late summer stragglers like Smooth Sumac. However, once fall fully arrives, it brings a rich harvest, especially known for its nuts. Black walnuts and acorns from oak trees are abundant, providing a hearty and nutritious foraging option. Tender leafy greens like wild lettuce and chickweed make a comeback, and Virginia pine needles become more aromatic, adding a unique flavor to various dishes. But the true star of the season is the wild American persimmon, whose sweet, jammy pulp captures fall's essence.

Imagine walking through an open meadow or along the sunny edges of a field in fall. You may come across American hazelnut trees, their nuts ready to be harvested. The rich, sweet fruit of the American persimmon hangs heavy on the branches, waiting to be picked. Apples, crabapples, and wild pears add to the fruity bounty, while nuts like hickory, beech, and butternut offer a nutritious snack. The vibrant berries of autumn olive and the tangy rose hips can be found along the edges of these sunny areas, adding color and flavor to your foraged meals.

The bounty continues in woodlands and partially shaded places. Beech nuts, black walnuts, and butternuts are plentiful. The inner bark and twigs of black birch can be used for tea or flavoring, while the roots of crinkleroot and cow parsnip seeds offer unique culinary opportunities. The vibrant berries of spicebush and the aromatic twigs of Virginia pine are found in these shaded areas, providing a sensory delight as you walk through the woods.

Fall brings opportunities to the seashore and coastal areas. Here, juniper berries are ripe and ready to be picked. Their distinctive flavor is perfect for seasoning dishes. Pennywort stems and flowers add a fresh, herbal note to salads, while red bay leaves can enhance the flavor of stews and soups. Saltwort and sea purslane leaves offer a salty, succulent bite, ideal for adding to your foraged feasts.

Wetlands, riverbanks, and lakesides are equally rewarding during fall. American lotus tubers provide a starchy, nutritious food source, while the seeds of pickerelweed add a crunchy texture to dishes. Wapato, known as duck potato, is another wetland treasure with tubers offering a rich, potato-like flavor.

Fall foraging requires some caution and preparation. The unpredictable weather means you must be ready for sudden changes. Poisonous plants are more prevalent in some areas, so proper identification is crucial. Additionally, larger wildlife like bears and deer are more active as they prepare for winter, so staying aware of your surroundings is vital.

Despite these challenges, fall is a season of abundance and variety. The cooler temperatures make foraging more comfortable, and the foliage's changing colors provide a beautiful backdrop for your outdoor adventures. The rich, earthy flavors of fall's bounty, from the sweet persimmons to the hearty nuts and aromatic herbs, make it a truly special time for foragers in the Southeast. As you gather and enjoy these wild edibles, you connect with nature's rhythms and foraging's timeless traditions.

# Winter

Winter in the Southeast, especially in January and February, brings the coldest weeks of the year. Despite the chill and often bleak landscapes, many wild edible plants withstand the weather and offer foragers a unique array of flavors and nutrients.

Imagine a cold, crisp day with the ground covered in frost. You step outside and find field garlic peeking through the cold soil. Its vibrant green shoots are a welcome sight, providing a flavor similar to chives or green onions. Field garlic brings a fresh, zesty kick to winter meals, whether sprinkled on soups or added to salads.

Chickweed is another winter gem. Picture finding this delicate plant, its small green leaves thriving despite the cold. On a bleak winter day, chickweed's raw green pea flavor is a delightful surprise, adding a burst of freshness to your foraged dishes.

In open meadows and sunny areas, several plants continue to thrive. The inner bark, twigs, and sap of black birch can be harvested and used to make tea or as a flavoring. Hickory bark offers a unique, smoky flavor, perfect for enhancing winter stews and broths. Hoary bittercress is another hardy plant found in these areas, adding a spicy note to winter salads with its peppery leaves and flowers.

Virginia pine needles become more aromatic in the cold, and their citrusy flavor can make teas or infused oils. Wintergreen leaves and berries are another winter staple with their distinctive minty taste, perfect for making refreshing teas or flavoring desserts.

In woodlands and partially shaded places, you can find similar treasures. The black birch's inner bark and twigs, chickweed, and field garlic are abundant in these cooler, shaded areas. Sassafras bark and roots, known for their root beer-like flavor, can be harvested and used to make flavorful teas or syrups. Spicebush twigs add a warming, spicy note to winter dishes, perfect for infusions and teas.

Coastal areas and seashore offer ripe juniper berries that are ready to be harvested during winter. With their piney, slightly sweet flavor, these berries are excellent for seasoning meats or making infused spirits like gin.

Wetlands, riverbanks, and lakesides hold winter treasures. American lotus tubers, starchy and nutritious, can be dug up from the cold, muddy ground. The inner bark, twigs, and black birch sap are found in these wet areas. Marsh marigold leaves, stalks, and flower buds can be foraged, providing a slightly bitter, cabbage-like flavor to winter dishes. Wapato, known as duck potato, offers tubers a taste similar to potatoes and can be cooked in numerous ways. Watercress thrives in these cold, wet environments, adding a fresh, spicy kick to your meals with its peppery leaves and stems.

Winter foraging requires more effort and preparation, but the rewards are significant. Dressing warmly and planning shorter foraging trips in cold weather is essential. Despite the challenges, winter foraging in the Southeast offers a unique experience. The hidden treasures connect you to the landscape profoundly, reminding you of nature's resilience and bounty even in the harshest conditions. As you gather these hardy plants, you bring the vibrant flavors of the wild into your home, making winter a season of discovery and delight.

Foraging in the Southeast is a dynamic and rewarding experience connecting you to nature's cycles. Each season offers distinct flavors and opportunities, making foraging a year-round adventure. As you continue to explore and gather wild edibles, remember to respect the environment and ensure sustainable practices. Always be prepared for each season's unique challenges, from sudden weather changes to wildlife encounters.

Each season demands specific preparations. Be ready for unpredictable weather and wildlife in spring. Summer requires protection against heat and insects. Fall is about timing your harvests to avoid competition with wildlife preparing for winter. Winter foraging demands warmth and short, efficient trips. Equip yourself accordingly with the proper clothing, tools, and knowledge.

Foraging in the Southeast is a dynamic journey through the seasons, offering more than food. It's an ongoing education, a sustainable practice, and a means to cultivate a deeper connection with nature. You can make foraging a rewarding and enriching part of your life by observing, learning, and respecting the environment. Embrace the seasonal rhythms and let each foraging trip teach you something new about the world around you and your place within it.

# Chapter 4: Wild Edible Plants of the Southeast

Have you ever struggled to identify plants, even the simplest ones? Don't worry. It happens to everyone. Recognizing plants can be tricky, especially if you plan to consume them. Maybe you've heard horrifying stories about foraging gone wrong, and now you're a bit scared to give it a try. It's completely understandable. However, don't let those fears hold you back. With the proper training and information, foraging can be a safe and rewarding experience.

This chapter will guide you through identifying and safely consuming wild edible plants in the Southeast. It will mainly consist of the easiest ones to identify so you're not too overwhelmed initially. You can study each plant's profile before your next foraging trip or keep it handy to look up plants while foraging.

# Greens and Shoots

Dandelion *(Taraxacum officinale)*

Dandelions are among the most familiar and accessible wild edible plants.[17]

Dandelions (*Taraxacum* spp.) are among the most familiar and accessible wild edible plants. Dandelions are easy to spot with their bright yellow flowers and deeply toothed, lance-shaped green leaves. These resilient plants can survive in a variety of environments, including lawns, meadows, and disturbed soils, making them one of the most widespread foraging finds. Moreover, they are nutritional powerhouses, rich in vitamins A, C, and K, and a host of minerals like calcium and iron.

When foraging for dandelions, look for their deeply lobed leaves, which form a circular rosette at the base. The tooth-like lobes point backwards, toward the rosette – a trait that can help distinguish the plant from lookalikes like the closely related chicory (*Cichorium intybus*). Another distinguishing feature is the hollow flower stalk or *scape*, which does not branch and which (unlike the leaves) exudes a bitter, milky sap when broken. Many plants in the sunflower or daisy family (Asteraceae) superficially resemble the dandelion, some quite closely – but the hollow, unbranched scapes of dandelions are unique to their genus. While the flowers and leaves are commonly used in salads and teas, the roots can also be roasted and ground to make a coffee substitute. Avoid plants growing in areas that may be exposed to pesticides or chemical fertilizers (farms, residential landscapes, sports fields, etc.).

### Lamb's Quarters *(Chenopodium album)*

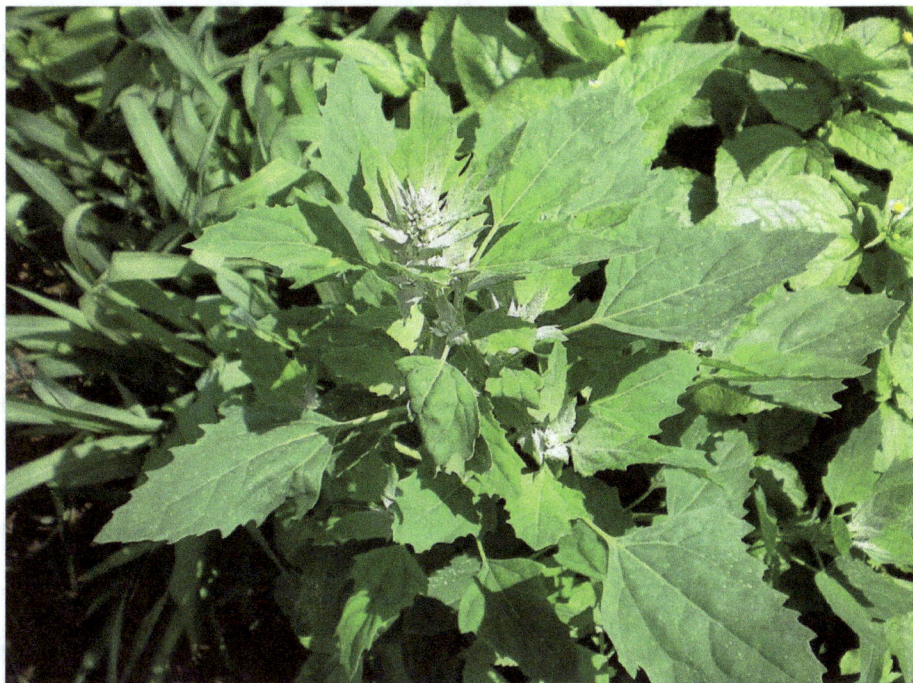

Lamb's quarters, known as wild spinach, are common among wild edible greens.[38]

Lamb's quarters (*Chenopodium album*), known as goosefoot, is among the most common and widespread plants on Earth, as well as a nutritious green that can be eaten raw or cooked. These plants are loaded with protein, calcium, iron, and vitamins, making them an excellent addition to your diet. They can be found in almost any sunny, disturbed habitat, often thriving on neglected or abandoned land. The leaves are diamond-shaped and toothed, and often bear a distinctive powdery white coating, especially on the underside (the specific epithet *album* refers to this coating).

To identify lamb's quarters, look for the floury or dusty white appearance on the, particularly the youngest leaves near the top of the plant. The plant is extraordinarily fast-growing, and can grow reach up to six feet tall in a few months, but only new growth should be harvested, as the leaves become tough and stringy as they age. These leaves can be used in salads, cooked as greens, or added to soups and stews. Raw leaves should be consumed in moderation as, like spinach greens, they contain oxalic acid, a chemical that interferes with the body's absorption of calcium (but is destroyed by cooking). Always harvest from clean areas, as lamb's quarters can absorb heavy metals from contaminated soils.

## Purslane *(Portulaca oleracea)*

Purslane is a succulent, low-growing plant with reddish stems and small, yellow flowers.[39]

Purslane is a succulent, low-growing plant with reddish stems and small yellow flowers. It is an exceptionally hardy plant, and thrives in the heat of summer, particularly in areas where thirstier competitors cannot survive: vacant lots, roadsides, and even sidewalks and parking lots. This tough plant is not merely a weed: it's packed with nutrients, including omega-3 fatty acids, antioxidants, and vitamins A, C, and E. The thick, fleshy leaves have a slightly tangy and salty taste, making them a delicious addition to salads and other dishes.

Identifying purslane is relatively straightforward. Look for its thick, succulent leaves and reddish stems, which are also edible. The leaves are small, oppositely arranged on the stem, and spoon- or spatula-shaped (widest near the tip). Beware of spotted or prostrate spurge (*Euphorbia maculata*), a toxic plant often found in similar habitats. Spotted spurge has reddish stems superficially similar to purslane, but without its succulent texture; the easiest way to distinguish the two plants is that spotted spurge exudes a milky sap from broken leaves or stems. Purslane is best harvested in the early morning when its leaves are plump and full of moisture.

## Wild Garlic *(Allium vineale)*

Wild garlic has thin, grass-like leaves and small, onion-like bulblets that pack a punch of flavor and nutrients.[50]

Wild garlic (*Allium vineale*), also known as crow garlic, is a delightful find for any forager. This plant has round, chive-like leaves and small, onion-like bulbs that pack a punch of flavor and nutrients. Wild garlic is rich in vitamin C and sulfur compounds, which have various health benefits, including boosting the immune system and reducing inflammation. You can find wild garlic growing abundantly in lawns, fields, and along roadsides, especially in areas with well-drained soil.

To identify wild garlic, look for its very long, in-rolled leaves, which often curl fancifully at the ends and emit a strong garlic smell. These rounded, tubular leaves are easy to distinguish from the flat, grass-like leaves of potentially dangerous look-alikes like crow poison (*Nothoscordum bivalve*) and fly poison (*Amianthum muscaetoxicum*), which also lack the strong garlicky aroma. As its name suggests, the leaves of wild garlic can be used in place of store-bought garlic. Both the true bulb (which forms below ground) and the aerial bulblets produced on the plant's stem can be used like green onions. Always ensure the area is free from contaminants before harvesting.

## Chickweed *(Stellaria media)*

Chickweed is a tender, bright green plant with small, star-shaped white flowers, adding a delicate touch to any dish.[51]

Chickweed is a tender, low-growing annual with tiny white flowers and edible greens that add a delicate touch to any dish. It emerges quite early in spring and thrives in moist, disturbed soils, often growing abundantly in partial shade. The plant dies soon after flowering, so don't wait to harvest – freeze any greens you can't use immediately, and enjoy them year-round in soups, stir-fries, or on their own. Chickweed is packed with vitamins A, C, and D and minerals like iron and calcium, making it a nutritious addition to your foraged greens.

To identify chickweed, look for its long, trailing stems and slightly fleshy opposite leaves. Look closer, and you'll see a single line of fine hairs running along the stems, a unique feature of chickweed. The flowers, though small, are also distinctive, with five deeply cleft V-shaped petals. Both the flowers and the stems are unique to chickweed, and will help distinguish it from the numerous inconspicuous annuals that superficially resemble it, like the toxic scarlet pimpernel (*Anagallis arvensis*), which is often found in similar habitats. Chickweed's delicate greens are best used fresh in salads, sandwiches, or as a garnish, but can also be used in place of spinach in soups and curries

# Edible Flowers

## Violet (*Viola* spp.)

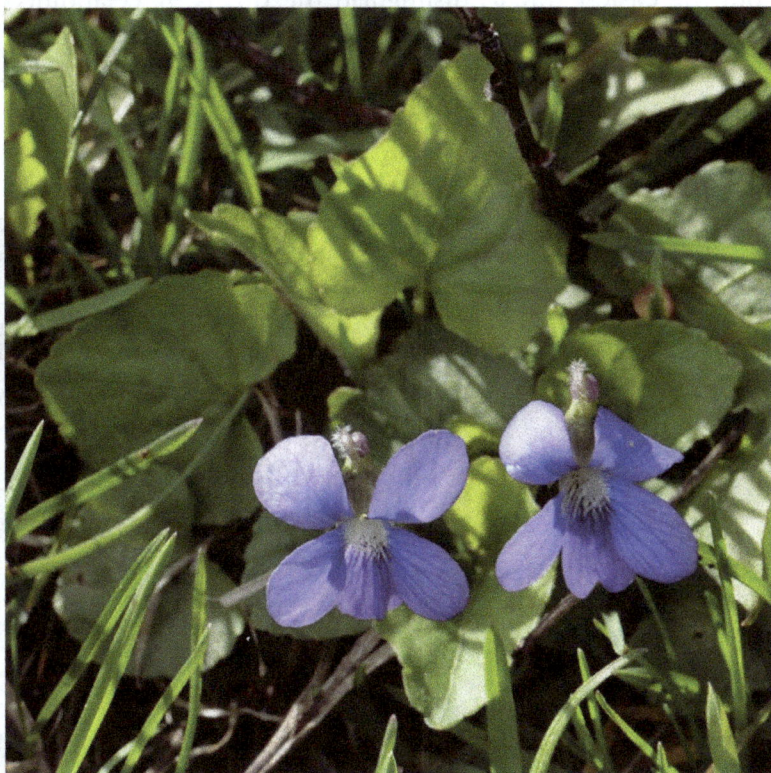

Missouri violets (*Viola sororia*) are among the most common wild violet in the Southeast.[88]

Violets (*Viola* spp.) are charming little flowers that bring a splash of color to your foraging basket. These delicate plants are quite variable in appearance, but most species have long-stemmed, heart-shaped leaves and distinctive zygomorphic (vertically symmetrical) white or purple flowers. Most violets are woodland plants, and outside of these habitats are often found in moist, shady areas like streambanks, parkland, and even lawns. Rich in vitamins A and C, violets not only add beauty but also a nutritional boost to your diet.

To identify violets, look for their distinctive heart-shaped leaves, which are borne on long petioles and often have scalloped margins. The flowers, which are borne on slender stalks only a few inches high, have five petals and can vary in color from deep purple to white; they have a distinctive, subtly sweet scent that can be difficult to detect. Beware of the common – and potentially toxic – lesser celandine (*Ficaria verna*), an exotic species with heart-shaped leaves similar to those of violets. Celandine leaves are generally rounded at the tips, rather than tapering to a point like those of violets, but the easiest way to distinguish the two is by celandine's bright yellow blooms – so beginning foragers should only harvest from plants with flowers. Violets can be added raw to salads, or used to make teas, syrups, and even candies. Ensure the area is free from pesticides before harvesting these lovely blooms.

### Redbud *(Cercis canadensis)*

Redbud trees are a beautiful sight in the spring, with their bright pink or purple flowers covering the branches before the leaves emerge.[88]

Redbud (*Cercis canadensis*) trees are a beautiful sight in the spring, with bright pink or purple flowers that, like cherry blossoms, emerge before the leaves. These trees are common in open woodlands and along streams throughout the eastern half of the continent from Texas to Pennsylvania. The flowers are not only beautiful but edible and nutritious, high in vitamin C and with a slightly tangy flavor delicious raw, fried, or pickled.

Redbuds are distinctive trees, and relatively easy to identify: the tree blooms before most other plants have even begun to wake from their winter slumber, with profuse pink, pea-like flowers that grow directly from the twigs and branches. The flowers are followed by heart-shaped leaves, which are unusual among legumes for being simple rather than compound. Redbuds are so distinctive that they cannot be said to have any real look-alikes, either edible or toxic, making them a safe choice for beginning foragers. The flowers can be eaten raw, fried like squash blossoms, or pickled, and add a splash of color and flavor to various dishes.

### Honeysuckle *(Lonicera* spp.*)*

Honeysuckle vines are well-known for their sweet, fragrant flowers, which bloom in summer.[54]

Honeysuckle (*Lonicera* spp.) vines are well-known for their sweet, fragrant flowers, which bloom profusely in summer. Though numerous species are native to North America, our most common species is probably Japanese honeysuckle (*L. japonica*), an introduced ornamental that climbs aggressively over fences, up trees, and among shrubs in sunny areas. The flowers are typically white or yellow and are rich in nectar, making them a favorite among foragers. Honeysuckle flowers are used in teas, syrups, and desserts.

To identify honeysuckle, look for its opposite leaves and tubular flowers, which have long, whisker-like stamens and emit a heady, sweet fragrance. A word of caution: although the flowers are safe to eat, all other parts of the plant – including the fruits – are potentially toxic, particularly when raw, and should be avoided. The flowers can be added to salads, lightly fried, or steeped in hot water to make a refreshing tea.

## Elder *(Sambucus nigra)*

The flowers and fruit of the elder are prized not only for their flavor but their therapeutic properties as well.[86]

Elderflowers come from the elder tree (*Sambucus nigra*) and are prized both for their delicate flavor and for their health benefits. These trees thrive in moist, open habitatas and are commonly found at the sunny edges of woodlands, from stream banks to fence rows and even roadsides. Elderflowers are rich in antioxidants and can be used to make syrups, cordials, and desserts.

Elderflowers, small individually, are easy to spot in late spring, when they bloom profusely in large, flat-topped clusters. The leaves of the elder are relatively distinctive as well, being both compound – each leaf containing 5, 7, or 9 lance-shaped leaflets – and oppositely arranged on the stem. Watch out for the common, highly toxic poison hemlock

(*Conium maculatum*), which also grows near water and has remarkably similar flowers and leaves. Unlike elder, hemlock – and a few of its close relatives, which are also toxic – is herbaceous, dying back to the ground each winter, while elder is a woody plant. Elderflowers should be harvested when fully open and can be used fresh or dried.

## Daylily (*Hemerocallis* spp.)

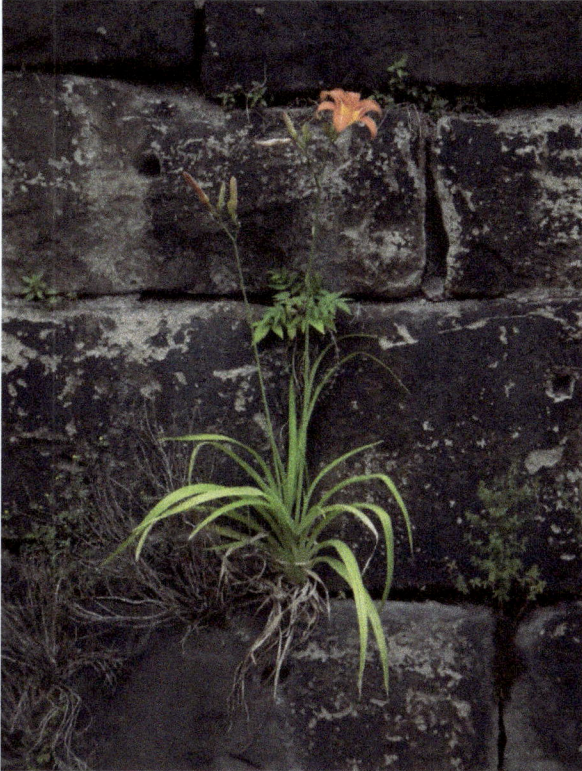

Daylilies are vibrant, trumpet-shaped flowers that come in a range of colors, including yellow, orange, and red.[56]

Daylilies (*Hemerocallis* spp.) are in the same family as true lilies (*Lillium* spp.), but their trumpet-shaped red, yellow, or orange flowers grow in clusters rather than singly, and last only a day or two (though plants may flower intermittently throughout the year). Introduced by Europeans as ornamental plants, they quickly escaped and naturalized, and today can be found not only in gardens but a variety of natural habitats, from stream banks and meadows to coastal sand dunes. Nearly the whole plant is edible, depending on the season: the young shoots and leaves are best harvested in spring, the potato-like tubers in autumn, and the flowers nearly year-round.

To identify daylilies, look for their distinctive trumpet-shaped, six-petaled flowers that bloom for only one day. The long, grass-like leaves emerge directly from the base, while the flowers grow on tall, leafless stems. Because daylilies are easily confused with related plants, many of which – like true lilies and irises – are poisonous, only harvest from plants with flowers, or which you have previously observed flowering. Daylilies are versatile in the kitchen and can be used in salads, soups, and stir-fries.

# Wild Berries

## Blueberries (*Vaccinium* spp.)

Blueberries are a favorite among foragers and gardeners alike.[37]

Blueberries (*Vaccinium* spp.) are a favorite among foragers and gardeners alike. While most supermarket blueberries come from a single species, the highbush blueberry (*Vaccinium corymbosum*), the genus is quite diverse, encompassing low-lying ground covers and thicket-forming shrubs, which may be known as huckleberries, farkleberries, or cranberries depending on the characteristics of the fruits. Blueberries and their cousins are found in a variety of habitats across the continent, but nearly always in acidic soils, especially marshy or boggy areas. They are packed with antioxidants, vitamins C and K, and fiber, making them a nutritious snack.

The most common species in the Southeast, the highbush blueberry, is a large shrub that can reach up to 10 feet in height, often forming dense thickets in good habitats. The leaves are elliptical, about an inch and a half long, and finely serrated along the margins. New leaves often have a reddish tinge, prefiguring the plant's vibrant fall color. The tiny, bell-shaped flowers are cream-colored and emerge in spring, later replaced by green berries that ripen to dark blue by the end of summer. Blueberries have no real lookalikes outside their genus, but may be confused with deerberries (*V. stamineum*) or farkleberries (*V. arboreum*), both of which are technically edible but have mealy and astringent fruits that are truly "for the birds" (and squirrels). Blueberries can be enjoyed fresh, in desserts, or made into jams and preserves.

### Blackberries (*Rubus* spp.)

Blackberries are a common sight in the Southeast, growing on thorny vines in woods, fields, and along fencerows.[38]

Blackberries, raspberries, and dewberries are part of a large and diverse genus (*Rubus*) collectively known as brambles. Their prickly canes are a common sight in the Southeast, sprawling over woods, fields, and fencerows, producing dark purple to black berries that are packed with vitamins C and K, fiber, and antioxidants. Blackberries thrive in sunny, disturbed areas, especially near water, from the edges of ponds and lakes to forest clearings and roadsides.

While the genus *Rubus* contains hundreds or even thousands of species, all share certain key characteristics: they grow on distinctive vine-like stems or *canes*, which are usually armed with prickles, and most have compound leaves with 3, 5, or 7 serrated leaflets (though a few have simple leaves). The flowers bloom in spring, and are white or pink in color, with five petals and numerous long stamens surrounding the pistils at their centers. Each pistil will eventually form one "pip" in the berries, which ripen in early to mid-summer; these are practically unmistakable, and among the safest choices for beginning foragers, as they only occur in brambles and are always edible.

## Elderberries *(Sambucus nigra)*

Elderberries are known for their immune-boosting properties.[30]

Elderberries are the fruits of the elder (see *Elderflowers*), small trees commonly found in moist, disturbed areas like woodland edges and streams. These small, dark purple to black berries are rich in vitamins A, B, and C, antioxidants, and flavonoids, and are thought to have immune-boosting, anti-inflammatory, and even antidiabetic effects.

Elderberries ripen from late summer to early fall, in large clusters with reddish stems. Beware of confusion with pokeweed (*Phytolacca americana*), a potentially toxic lookalike which also has deep purple berries on reddish stems. Fortunately, pokeweed's large, simple leaves and annual growth habit – its red stems are never woody – make it easy to distinguish from elder, provided you take the time to examine the plant closely. Raw elderberries, especially before they are fully ripe, contain toxic compounds that can cause serious illness, so berries should always be cooked thoroughly before consumption. Once properly processed, however, they have a complex flavor excellent in jam, baked goods, or syrup.

## Maypop *(Passiflora incarnata)*

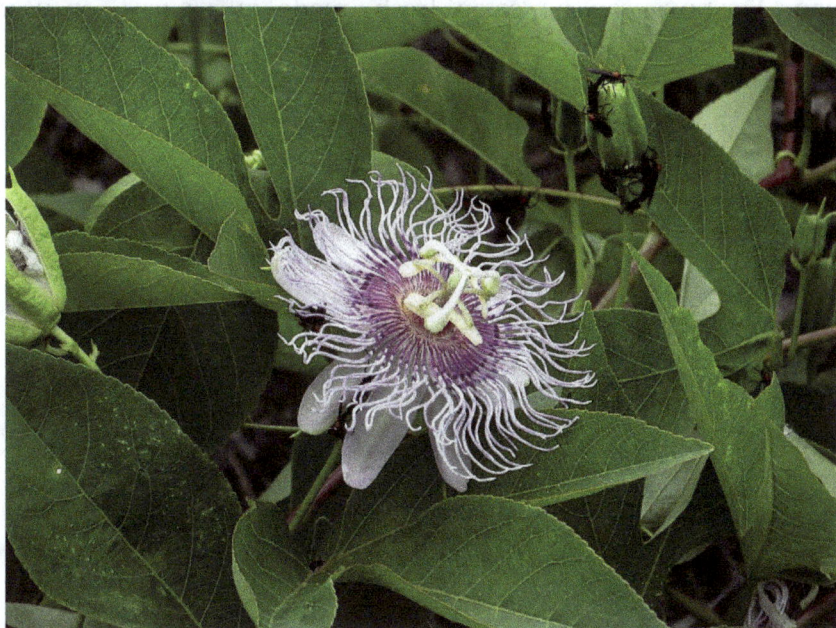

Maypop, also known as passion fruit, is a unique and exotic-looking berry found in the Southeast.[40]

Maypop (*Passiflora incarnata*), commonly known as passionflower or passion vine, is a unique and exotic-looking vine found across the Southeast. The unusual lilac flowers, which held complex symbolic significance for early Spanish settlers, ripen into large green fruits about the size and shape of an egg, which turn yellow inside and out when ripe.

While its aesthetic qualities have made it a opular ornamental, maypop is also a hardy native species, growing in fields, along roadsides, and in open woods, and often thriving on dry or poor soils. The fruit is rich in vitamins A and C and has a delightful tropical flavor.

To identify maypop, look for climbing vines with distinctive three-lobed leaves, which have distinctive nectar-producing glands at their bases. The large, showy flowers bloom throughout the heat of summer, and have a distinctive corona of fine purplish tendrils. The fruits are green when immature and turn yellow as they ripen, though some ripe fruits never fully lose their greenish coloring. When in doubt, cut a fruit open and examine the pulp: unripe fruits have white, opaque pulp, while the pulp of ripe fruits is yellowish and translucent. While passion vine has no true lookalikes, the wild yellow passionflower (*Passiflora lutea*) has similar, though much smaller, flowers and fruits. The latter are perfectly edible, but probably not worth harvesting, as each fruit is about the size of a soybean. Maypops can be eaten fresh, made into juices, or used in desserts.

# Nuts and Seeds

**Pecans** *(Carya illinoinensis)*

Pecans are encased in a hard, brown shell within a green husk that splits open when the nuts are ripe.[41]

Few wild foods are as quintessentially Southern as the pecan (*Carya illinoensis*), which are common across the Southeast but popular worldwide. Pecan trees are enormous, stately trees, and like deep, fertile soil; in the wild, they are most often found in floodplains and river bottoms, but you're equally likely to encounter them in parks and yards, and cultivated trees often produce larger and more flavorful nuts. The nuts – technically *drupes* like peaches or cherries – have subtly-patterned brown and black shells, and are encased in a leathery green husk that turns dark brown and splits into four sections as the nut within ripens. They are packed with healthy fats, protein, fiber, and essential vitamins and minerals, making them a nutritious, tasty snack.

To identify pecan trees, look for large, spreading trees with flaky or scaly gray bark and compound leaves with 9-17 leaflets. The flowers are produced on long catkins in spring, which eventually ripen into nuts that are nearly impossible to confuse with any other species. Hickory nuts (*Carya* spp.), though closely related, are rounder and stouter than pecans, with much thicker husks and wrinkly beige shells similar to walnuts (*Juglans* spp.); they are also edible, though some species are unpalatably bitter. Pecans can be enjoyed fresh, roasted, or used in baking and cooking.

## Acorns (*Quercus* spp.*)*

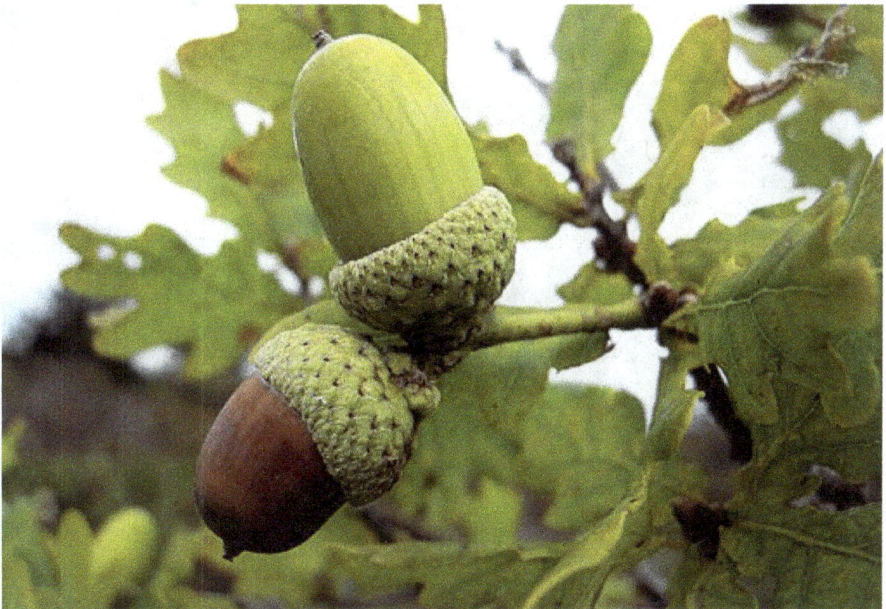

Acorns are the nuts of oak trees, common throughout the Southeast.[48]

Acorns are the nuts of oak trees (*Quercus* spp.), which are common to temperate forests around the world. These nuts are encased in a tough, slightly flexible brown shell with a characteristic scaly cap or cupule. Oaks can be found in woodlands, parks, and urban areas almost everywhere in North America outside of the driest desert regions; in the Southeast, some of the most common species are white oak (*Q. alba*), red oak (*Q. rubra*), chinkapin oak (*Q. muehlenbergii*) and bur oak (*Q. macrocarpa*). They are a rich source of carbohydrates, fats, and protein, but contain bitter tannins that must be leached via boiling or soaking before consumption.

In general, acorns from oaks with wavy, lobed leaves (the so-called "white oaks") have lower tannin content and a milder flavor than those of species with spiky or bristly leaves (commonly known as "red oaks"). Look for the acorns in autumn, and inspect them carefully: ripe acorns should be easy to pull from their caps, and shouldn't have any cracks or holes, which are generally signs of mold or insect infestation. However, sprouted acorns are an exception to this rule, and some foragers say they have the best flavor, as sprouting converts the carbohydrates in the acorn into sugar. To prepare acorns, shell them and boil them in at least two changes of water to leach the tannins. They will turn the water brown as they leach out, so the acorns are ready when they no longer discolor the water. Once leached, they can be roasted and eaten like chestnuts, or dried and ground into flour for baking.

### Hickory Nuts (*Carya* spp.)

Hickory nuts are another wild edible found in the Southeast, growing on hickory trees that thrive in forests and woodlands.⁴

60

Hickories (*Carya* spp.) are closely related to pecans (*C. illinoensis*, and like pecans thrive in riparian forests and woodlands. The nuts resemble pecans somewhat, but are more spherical in shape and have much thicker husks and shells. Hickory nuts are rich in healthy fats, protein, and vitamins, making them a nutritious food.

Not all hickories produce edible nuts, though opinions differ on which species qualify; perhaps the most common and popular species is the shagbark hickory (*Carya ovata*), easily identified by its large size and shaggy, exfoliating bark, which peels away from the trunk as it ages. The leaves of shagbark hickory look much like pecan leaves, but generally have only 5 leaflets, while pecan leaves have 11 or 13. Hickory *nuts* are less likely than hickory *trees* to be confused with pecans, but beginning foragers may mistake black walnuts (*Juglans nigra*) for underripe hickory nuts. Black walnuts are related to pecans and hickories, but their husks are much thicker and do not split when ripe. Black walnuts are also edible, but a lot more work to process. Hickory nuts can be used in place of or alongside pecans and walnuts, and can be ground and simmered to make "hickory milk", a beverage popular among indigenous peoples and early settlers of the Southeast.

## Chestnuts (*Castanea* spp.)

The Allegheny chinkapin (*Castanea pumila*) is the most commonly encountered species of chestnut in the Southeast."

Chestnuts are members of the same family as oaks (*Quercus*) and beeches (*Fagus*), and like these species are commonly found in forests and woodlands in the Southeast. The American chestnut (*C. dentata*) once dominated eastern North American forests, but was decimated in the early 20th century by a fungal infection known as chestnut blight, from which it has have never truly recovered. However, the dwarf chestnut or chinkapin (*C. pumila*) has managed to resist chestnut blight, and remains a common understory species in Southeastern forests.

To identify chestnuts: look for the long, serrated leaves and the spiky burrs that contain the nuts. These split open at maturity to reveal shiny brown nuts somewhat reminiscent of acorns. Be cautious of horse chestnuts (*Aesculus hippocastanum*), which are toxic and have a similar appearance. Unlike true chestnuts, horse chestnuts have palmately compound leaves, with five or seven leaflets radiating from a central point like an open hand. Chestnuts must be cooked before eating, and can be roasted, boiled, or used in stuffing and desserts.

## Black Walnuts (*Juglans nigra*)

**Black walnuts are encased in a thick, green husk that turns black and decays when the nuts are ripe.[46]**

Black walnuts (*Juglans nigra*) are the flavorful nuts of the black walnut tree, a relative of hickories and pecans (*Carya*) as well as common walnuts (*J. regia*). The tree has dark, ridged bark and compound leaves similar to pecan leaves, which emit a distinctive, pungent smell when crushed. The nuts are encased in a thick, green husk that darkens to brown and then black as the nuts ripen within. Black walnut trees are commonly found in forests and woodlands, especially along streams. They are rich in healthy fats, protein, and antioxidants.

The easiest way to identify black walnuts is to look for the distinctive nuts scattered around the ground; while the husks decay relatively quickly, the hard, ridged shells take far longer to break down and are an indication that you're near (or perhaps underneath) a black walnut tree. Younger specimens of the closely related pecan (*Carya illinoiensis*) can be mistaken for black walnut, but are easily distinguished by their leaves: pecan leaves usually have 9 or 11 leaflets, while black walnut leaves have 15 or more.

More challenging than identifying black walnuts is shelling them, especially as the green husks contain a juice that can stain your hands for days. Methods range from pounding the nuts through a piece of PVC to running them over with your car – or if you're not in a hurry, you can simply leave them outside and wait for the husks to decay naturally. Once husked and freed from their shells (a bench vise works well for this) they can be eaten raw, roasted, or used in baking and cooking.

# Roots and Tubers

### Wild Yams (*Dioscorea* spp.)

The Chinese yam (*Dioscorea polystachya*) is among the most common species of wild yam in the Southeast. It is sometimes called "air potato" for the aboveground tubers it produces, but these are generally not eaten."

Wild yams *(Dioscorea* spp.) are climbing, perennial vines with starchy tubers. Most species occur in the tropics, but a handful of species can be found throughout the Southeast, generally in moist forests and at the edges of wetlands. Their stems, which can reach 30 feet long, are often grooved or winged, and their heart-shaped leaves resemble those of wild sweet potato *(Ipomoea pandurata)*, although the species aren't closely related. While they're not showy plants, even when in bloom, wild yams are still fairly easy to recognize, as their leaves have distinctively parallel, unbranched veins – similar to grass or lily leaves. (They're actually more closely related to both of these plants than they are to sweet potatoes!) The tubers look similar to new potatoes, both in size and color. Wild yams are rich in carbohydrates, fiber, and vitamins, making them a valuable food source for foragers, but must be cooked thoroughly to remove toxic saponins.

To identify wild yams, look for vines with angled or winged stems and heart-shaped leaves with parallel veins. Although the genus has no real lookalikes, note that not all species are edible, and several are toxic. In North America, species with opposite leaves have edible tubers, while species with alternate leaves do not – so before you harvest, check to make sure you've found an edible species. The most common of these are the introduced Chinese yam *(D. polystachya)*, and purple yam *(D. alata)*. Wild yams can be boiled, roasted, or mashed just like sweet potatoes, and are excellent in soups, stews, and casseroles.

## Jerusalem Artichokes *(Helianthus tuberosus)*

Jerusalem artichokes, or sunchokes, are edible tubers growing in sunny fields, along roadsides, and in disturbed soils.[47]

Despite its name, Jerusalem artichoke (*Helianthus tuberosus*) isn't an artichoke at all but a species of sunflower with edible tubers that can be cooked and eaten like potatoes. Native to the Great Plains, it's naturalized throughout the eastern Noth America and can be found growing in sunny fields, roadsides, and other disturbed soils. The knobby, brown-skinned tubers have crisp, white flesh and a nutty, slightly sweet flavor that's somewhat reminiscent of artichoke hearts. Jerusalem artichokes are rich in carbohydrates, fiber, and potassium, making them a nutritious addition to your diet.

To identify Jerusalem artichokes, look for tall, sunflower-like plants with lance-shaped leaves and yellow flowers that bloom in late summer or early fall. The tubers are typically found just below the soil surface and can be dug up with a shovel or garden fork. The best time to harvest tubers is just after the first frost in early winter, after the plants have died back to the ground. Their only real lookalikes are common or annual sunflowers (*H. annuus*), which have much broader, heart-shaped leaves and lack the distinctive tubers. Jerusalem artichokes can be eaten raw or cooked and used in salads, soups, and stir-fries.

### Burdock *(Arctium* spp.*)*

Burdock is a biennial plant with large, heart-shaped leaves and deep, fleshy roots that grow in fields, waste areas, and along roadsides.[48]

Burdock is a biennial plant with large, heart-shaped leaves and a deep, fleshy taproot that grows in fields, roadsides, and other neglected places.

The root, which can reach two to three feet in length, is brown on the outside and white on the inside, with a crisp texture and a pungent yet sweet flavor, which can be mellowed by chopping the root and soaking the pieces in water. Burdock roots are rich in carbohydrates, fiber, and antioxidants, making them a nutritious addition to your diet.

Burdock spends its first year as a rosette of large, broad leaves, similar in appearance to rhubarb or chard. In its second year, the plant bolts, sometimes reaching eight feet high and topped with purple flowers that bloom throughout the summer. Only the roots of first-year plants are suitable for eating; these can be dug up with a long-bladed shovel, or if you have one, a post hole digger (cut the leaves back first). Burdocks have no real lookalikes; dock (*Rumex* spp.), the plant's namesake, has somewhat similar leaves and produces a taproot like burdock's but is much smaller. Burdock roots can be boiled, roasted, stir-fried or even pickled, and are a great addition to soups, stews, and teas.

### Wild Sweet Potato *(Ipomoea pandurata)*

Closely related to the cultivated sweet potato (*Ipomoea batatas*), wild sweet potato (*I. pandurata*) is a native perennial vine reaching up to 30 feet in length, with heart-shaped leaves that are often tinged with purple. The trailing stems sprout from tubers, belowground storage organs that taste a lot like their supermarket cousins, though they're generally longer and skinnier. The flowers are large, white, and trumpet-shaped, with a pink or purple spot at the very center.

To identify sweet potatoes, look for trailing vines with heart-shaped leaves that spread across the ground. The tubers are typically harvested in the fall

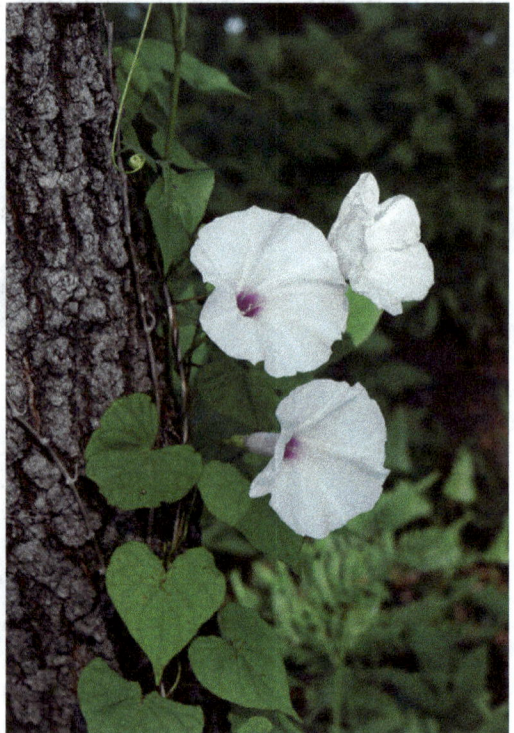

Wild sweet potato (*I. pandurata*) is closely related to morning glories, and has similar flowers, which are distinctively white with purple throats.[46]

and can be dug up carefully with a shovel or garden fork; tubers from young plants, while smaller, have a superior flavor and texture to larger, older specimens. Wild sweet potatoes can be confused with other species in the morning glory family, many of which are toxic; tievine (*I. cordatotriloba*) and bindweed (*Convolvulus* spp.) are two of the most common, but can be distinguished by their flowers: tievine has magenta flowers, while bindweed has pure white flowers with no coloring at the center. Sweet potatoes can be baked, boiled, roasted, or mashed and used in a variety of dishes, from soups and stews to pies and desserts.

As you start your foraging journey, always prioritize safety and sustainability. Take time to correctly identify each plant using multiple reliable sources, and be cautious of potential look-alikes and poisonous counterparts. Respect nature's abundance by harvesting responsibly and leaving enough plants to regenerate and support local ecosystems. With the knowledge gained from this chapter, you're well-equipped to start looking for basic, easily recognizable plants.

# Chapter 5: Mushrooms of the Southeast

Have you ever thought about foraging for mushrooms? No, not the kind that makes you see pink elephants, but the ones you can eat! Mushrooms are like nature's little surprises, hiding under leaves and peeking out from tree trunks. However, don't be fooled. Not all mushrooms are made equal. Before you start plucking, you must learn a few things, such as how to distinguish good mushrooms from bad and why paying attention is crucial. After all, no one wants to bite into a poisonous mushroom by mistake.

## The Basics

Start with the basics of mushroom anatomy. Picture a mushroom – it's not only a cute cap on a stem. There's much more to it. Mushrooms have different parts, like the cap, stem, gills, and spores. These parts are essential to help you identify them correctly.

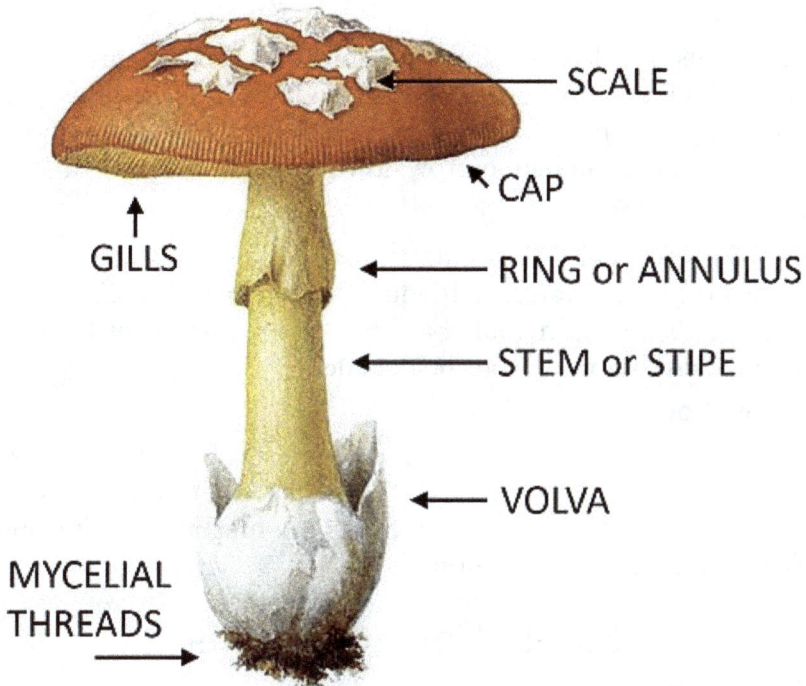

Mushrooms have different parts, like the cap, stem, gills, and spores.[50]

Now, why is accurate identification so important? It's simple – mushrooms can be friends or foes. Some are tasty treats, while others are downright dangerous. Knowing the differences can mean a delightful meal or a trip to the emergency room.

So, before you rush into the woods with your mushroom basket, take this word of caution: not all mushrooms are safe to eat. Some can make you seriously ill or worse. This is why it's essential to approach mushroom foraging carefully and cautiously. Always double-check your identifications, and when in doubt, leave it out!

# Mushroom Identification Techniques

## Observe

Ah, the art of observation – sounds simple, right? Wrong! It is the most crucial step, and you must put all your focus into it. Unless you want to end up in the emergency room accidentally, take a moment to observe the mushroom in front of you. Notice its color, shape, size, and texture. Does it have gills, pores, or teeth? These little details provide valuable clues about the mushroom's identity.

### Spore Prints

Spore prints are like nature's signature – each mushroom species leaves behind a unique pattern of spores. To make a spore print, place the mushroom cap on a piece of paper and wait. The color of the spores that drop onto the paper can help narrow down your mushroom's identity.

### Smell Test

Close your eyes and take a sniff – the nose knows! Many mushrooms have distinct odors that can help in identification. Some smell sweet, while others are earthy or even foul. Pay attention to the scent and see if it matches any descriptions in your field guide.

### Location, Location, Location

Like in real estate, location matters with mushrooms. Different species have specific habitats they prefer, whether under oak trees, in grassy fields, or on decaying logs. Note where you found the mushroom – it could be a valuable clue for later identification.

# Safety Considerations

### The Golden Rule

Here's the golden rule of mushroom foraging: when in doubt, don't eat it. It's better to be safe than sorry with mushrooms. If you're unsure about a mushroom's identity, leave it be. It's not worth the risk of ingesting something toxic.

### Toxic Look-Alikes

Mushrooms have their doppelgangers, too – toxic look-alikes that can fool even the most experienced foragers. For example, the deadly galerina closely resembles the beloved honey mushroom. Knowing how to distinguish between edible mushrooms and their toxic counterparts is crucial for your own safety.

### Responsible Foraging Practices

When foraging for mushrooms, practicing responsible foraging to minimize the environmental impact is essential. Avoid trampling delicate habitats, and only harvest mushrooms in moderation. Leave some behind to ensure the continued growth and reproduction of mushroom populations.

### Educate Yourself

One of the best ways to stay safe while foraging for mushrooms is to educate yourself. Take time to learn about the mushrooms native to your area, their habitats, and their identifying features. Attend workshops, join forays, and connect with experienced foragers to expand your knowledge and skills.

### Toxicity Testing

If you're unsure about a mushroom's edibility, there are ways to test its toxicity before consuming it. Some foragers use a small nibble and wait method, while others prefer chemical tests like the iodine test. However, these methods are not foolproof and should only be used by experienced foragers.

# Mushroom Profiles

## Chanterelle *(Cantharellus* spp.*)*

Chanterelles have a delicate, fruity aroma reminiscent of apricots, making them a delight to the senses.[51]

These trumpet-shaped mushrooms have a vibrant golden to orange hue, a velvety-smooth cap, and a gently curved stem. Chanterelles have a delicate, fruity aroma reminiscent of apricots, which is both a delight to the senses and a helpful identifying feature. You'll often find them nestled among the leaf litter in hardwood forests, especially near oak and beech trees. Look for the distinctive folds on the cap's underside, which look like gills but are thicker and usually forked; these are a key identifier, helping to distinguish them from false chanterelles.

Chanterelles are liked for their rich, nutty flavor and meaty texture, making them a favorite ingredient in gourmet dishes ranging from risottos to pasta sauces. Harvesting chanterelles can be a rewarding experience, but it's essential to exercise caution and correctly identify them before consumption.

## Morel *(Morchella* spp.*)*

These cone-shaped mushrooms feature a distinctive honeycomb-like cap with deep, irregular pits and ridges that give them their characteristic appearance.[53]

These cone-shaped mushrooms feature a distinctive chambered, honeycomb-like cap with deep, irregular pits and ridges that give them a unique appearance. Cut one in half and you'll see that the stems are entirely hollow, another key trait in distinguishing them from potentially toxic lookalikes. Morels typically emerge in spring, often in burned or disturbed areas like recently logged forests or wildfire sites. Morels are prized for their earthy, nutty flavor and meaty texture, which intensifies when cooked. However, caution is advised, as a number of related species, some of them toxic or unpalatable, can be mistaken for true morels.

When foraging for morels, carefully inspect each specimen for a chambered cap and hollow stem: false morels have wrinkly caps, and while their stems may contain empty air pockets, they are not truly hollow. With their transient nature and irresistible flavor, morels are a coveted find for mushroom enthusiasts and a true symbol of the changing seasons in the wild.

### Chicken of the Woods *(Laetiporus sulphureus)*

You may stumble upon a vibrant patch of chicken of the woods if you're lucky during your mushroom forays. These striking mushrooms emerge in large, shelf-like clusters with overlapping layers, which are bright orange or yellow in color and have a flavor and texture remarkably like that of cooked chicken (hence the name). They're typically found growing on decaying hardwood trees, such as oak or cherry, and are most abundant in the summer and fall months. Chicken of the Woods is prized for its meaty flavor and texture, making it a popular choice for vegetarian dishes like stir-fries and tacos.

Although no other species closely resemble chicken of the woods, it must be cooked thoroughly before eating, as it can cause gastrointestinal upset if consumed raw.

### Hen of the Woods *(Grifola frondosa)*

A true forest gem, Hen of the Woods is a sight to behold with its large, fan-shaped clusters and unique, layered appearance.[53]

A true forest gem, Hen of the Woods is a sight to behold with its large, fan-shaped clusters and unique, layered appearance. These mushrooms grow at the base of oak, beech, and other hardwood trees in the fall, often forming impressive displays resembling a hen's plumage – hence the name. Hen of the Woods has a tender, meaty texture and a savory, umami flavor that intensifies when cooked. They're best harvested when young and tender, as older specimens can become tough and unpalatable.

Hen of the Woods is prized for its culinary versatility and is typically used in soups, stews, and risottos. However, exercising caution when foraging for hen of the woods is essential, as you could experience gastrointestinal upset after consuming certain specimens.

### Oyster Mushroom *(Pleurotus ostreatus)*

Oyster mushrooms are a common sight in the wild, often growing on dead or dying hardwood trees in large clusters. They have a distinctive kidney- or oyster-shaped cap with a smooth, velvety texture and delicate, ivory-colored flesh. Oyster mushrooms are prized for their mild, slightly sweet flavor and tender texture, making them a versatile ingredient in various dishes. Look for them in spring and fall months, especially after periods of rain.

Oyster mushrooms are relatively easy to identify and are generally considered safe for beginning foragers, but always exercise caution when foraging for mushrooms of any kind, and consult an expert before consuming any mushroom for the first time. Proper identification is essential. With their delicate flavor and satisfying texture, oyster mushrooms are a delightful addition to soups, stir-fries, and pasta dishes, adding depth and complexity to every bite.

### Lion's Mane *(Hericium erinaceus)*

With its shaggy, white appearance, the lion's mane is one of the most distinctive mushrooms you'll encounter in the wild."

With its shaggy, white appearance, the lion's mane is one of the most distinctive mushrooms you'll encounter in the wild. These fascinating fungi grow on hardwood trees, often resembling cascading icicles or a lion's mane – hence the name. Lion's mane is prized for its unique, seafood-like flavor and meaty texture, making it a popular choice for vegetarian and vegan dishes. Look for them in the fall and even well into winter, especially in hardwood forests and wooded areas. Lion's mane is best harvested when young and tender, as older specimens can be infested with insect larvae. They're commonly used in dishes like stir-fries, soups, and risotto.

The bizarre, shaggy appearance of lion's mane makes it practically unmistakable, but it's also relatively rare, so don't expect to find one on your first foray. In addition to their culinary uses, lion's mane mushrooms are believed to have medicinal properties. Traditional Chinese medicine often uses them to improve cognitive function, boost the immune system, and support overall health.

### Reishi *(Ganoderma* spp.*)*

Reishi mushrooms are revered not for their flavor but for their medicinal properties, which were so highly regarded in ancient China that the reishi was called the "mushroom of immortality". These woody, shelf-like mushrooms grow on hardwood trees and are easily identified by their scarlet caps, which have a shiny, lacquered appearance . Reishi mushrooms have a bitter taste and tough texture, so they're not generally eaten but processed into teas, tinctures, and ither supplements. They are reputed to have various health benefits, particularly to the immune system, and have been used in traditional Chinese medicine for centuries to promote longevity, reduce stress, and improve overall health.

When foraging for reishi mushrooms, look for them on dead or decaying hardwood trees, especially oak, maple, and beech. They typically appear as large, woody conks that are shiny and reddish-brown above and white below. Reishi has few lookalikes, and none that are known to be toxic, but always ask for a second opinion, and consult your doctor before taking any supplement.

## Shaggy Mane *(Coprinus comatus)*

The shaggy mane is a curious mushroom with a distinctive appearance and ephemeral nature.[55]

The shaggy mane is a distinctive and extremely ephemeral mushroom. These tall, slender mushrooms emerge with white, bell-shaped caps covered in shaggy scales and bearing delicate white or pink gills beneath. In as little as a few hours, however, their appearance quickly changes, as they blacken and melt, leaving behind only a pool of inky goo. Shaggy manes are common in lawns, parks, and even mulched garden beds in the spring and fall months. They have a mild, nutty flavor and tender texture when young, but can still be eaten even after they begin to deliquesce; although they don't look especially appetizing, many foragers claim that their flavor improves as they age.

Identifying shaggy mane mushrooms is relatively straightforward due to their unique appearance. They have a tall, cylindrical or bell-shaped cap covered in fine scales, giving them a distinctly "hairy" appearance. The shaggy mane's gills are initially white but turn black and liquefy as the mushroom matures, eventually resembling a mass of black ink. Shaggy manes typically grow in clusters in grassy areas, lawns, and meadows near compost piles or decaying organic matter.

When foraging for shaggy mane mushrooms, harvesting them when they're young and fresh to enjoy their delicate flavor and texture fully is essential. Look for specimens with firm, unblemished caps and cook them as soon as possible, as they can quickly deteriorate once picked.

## Turkey Tail *(Trametes versicolor)*

Turkey tail mushrooms are a common sight in forests and woodlands, growing on dead or decaying wood. They have a fan-shaped cap with concentric rings of various colors, resembling a turkey's tail feathers – hence the name. Like reishi mushrooms, turkey tail mushrooms are valued not for their culinary value but are prized for their medicinal properties. They're believed to have immune-boosting and anticancer effects, and can be dried and ground into powder, which can be encapsulated or made into tea. Look for them year-round, especially on fallen logs and stumps, but properly identify them before use.

Identifying turkey tail mushrooms is relatively easy due to their distinctive appearance. They have a fan-shaped cap with concentric bands of various colors, including brown, tan, white, and occasionally blue. The underside of the turkey tail cap features tiny pores instead of gills, which release spores as the mushroom matures. Turkey tail mushrooms typically grow in large clusters on dead or decaying hardwood trees, especially oak, maple, and beech.

When foraging turkey tail mushrooms, only harvest fresh specimens that are firm but flexible, and avoid those with signs of decay or insect infestation. Turkey tail mushrooms can be harvested year-round, but they're most abundant in the fall and spring months when conditions are favorable for their growth.

## Coral Mushroom *(Ramaria* spp.*)*

Coral mushrooms are a fascinating group of mushrooms with a distinctive coral-like appearance. They have branching, coral-like structures instead of the typical cap and stem morphology. Coral mushrooms come in various colors, ranging from white and yellow to orange and pink. While some coral mushrooms are edible and prized for their delicate flavor, others are toxic and should be avoided. Proper identification when foraging coral mushrooms is essential to ensure you harvest the edible species.

Identifying coral mushrooms can be challenging due to their variability in color and shape, but there are a few key features to look for when foraging. Edible coral mushrooms typically have a branching, coral-like structure with smooth, unblemished branches and a firm, fleshy texture. In contrast, toxic coral mushrooms may have slimy or sticky branches, a foul odor, or a bitter taste when cooked.

When foraging coral mushrooms, harvesting them when they're young and fresh for the best flavor and texture is essential. Look for specimens with firm, unblemished branches and avoid mushrooms showing signs of decay or contamination. Coral mushrooms typically grow in mixed woodlands and coniferous forests, especially after rain or high-humidity periods.

Coral mushrooms are prized for their delicate flavor and unique texture, making them a versatile ingredient in various culinary dishes. They can be sautéed with garlic and herbs, added to omelets or frittatas, or grilled and served as a flavorful side dish. Coral mushrooms pair well with a wide range of ingredients, including poultry, seafood, and vegetables, making them a popular choice for vegetarian and omnivorous diets.

## Black Trumpet *(Craterellus cornucopioides)*

Black trumpets are a prized find for mushroom foragers, known for their distinctive trumpet-like shape and deep, smoky flavor.[66]

Black trumpets are a prized find for mushroom foragers, known for their distinctive trumpet-like shape and deep, smoky flavor. These funnel-shaped mushrooms are typically found in hardwood forests, growing in mossy areas or near decaying logs. Black trumpets have a dark brown to black color and delicate, thin flesh. They're prized for their rich, earthy flavor, which intensifies when dried, making them a popular choice for soups, sauces, and risotto.

Identifying black trumpet mushrooms is relatively easy due to their distinctive appearance and habitat preferences. They have a funnel-shaped cap with a fluted edge and a smooth, velvety texture. Black trumpets typically grow in groups on the forest floor, near decaying logs or mossy areas. They're most abundant in summer and fall months, especially after rainfall or periods of high humidity.

Black trumpet mushrooms are prized for their rich, earthy flavor and delicate texture, making them a favorite among mushroom enthusiasts. They can be sautéed with garlic and herbs, added to soups and stews, or dried and rehydrated for later use. Black trumpets pair well with a wide range of ingredients, including poultry, game meats, and wild mushrooms, making them a versatile ingredient in various culinary dishes.

### Yellowfoot *(Craterellus tubaeformis)*

Yellowfoot mushrooms, known as winter chanterelles, are a delightful find for mushroom foragers, adding a burst of color and flavor to winter landscapes. These trumpet-shaped mushrooms have a golden-yellow to orange-brown cap with a depression in the center, and a hollow, cylindrical stem. Yellowfoot mushrooms typically grow in clusters on the forest floor, in mossy areas, or near decaying logs. They're prized for their delicate, nutty flavor and firm, meaty texture, making them a popular choice for soups, stews, and pasta dishes.

Identifying yellowfoot mushrooms is relatively easy due to their distinctive appearance and habitat preferences. They have a trumpet-shaped cap with a central depression, a wavy, irregular edge and a smooth, velvety texture. Yellowfoot mushrooms typically grow in clusters on the forest floor, in mossy areas, or near decaying logs. They're most abundant in the winter months, especially after rainfall or during high-humidity periods.

## Russula *(Russula* spp.*)*

Russula mushrooms are a diverse group known for their vibrant colors and brittle texture.[57]

Russula mushrooms are a diverse group known for their vibrant colors and brittle flesh. They have smooth, flat-topped or upturned caps that are often brightly colored (typically red) and white to cream-colored gills that are attached to the stem (but do not extend down it). The stem itself, like the rest of the mushroom, are quite brittle, and can be broken like a piece of chalk, Russula mushrooms are found in a range of habitats, but are most common in woodlands due to the symbiotic relationships they form with trees. Some russula species are edible and prized for their mild flavor, others are toxic, though these generally produce only mild gastrointestinal symptoms. Because the genus contains so few highly toxic species, most foragers use a simple "taste test" to check the edibility of russula: break off a small piece of the cap, chew it up, and spit it out – a mild, sweet, or mushroomy flavor indicates an edible species, while an acrid, spicy, or otherwise unpleasant taste is a sign of a toxic species.

## Porcini *(Boletus edulis)*

Porcini mushrooms, known as king boletes, are highly prized not only for their rich, nutty flavor and meaty texture but because they cannot be cultivated – the only way to eat fresh porcinis is to go out and pick them yourself! They have thick, bulbous stems covered in net-like wrinkles, and distinctive reddish-brown to dark brown caps that look like dinner rolls. Like all boletes, the underside of the porcini's cap is covered with tiny tubes instead of gills. Porcini mushrooms are typically found in mixed woodlands and coniferous forests, especially under oak, pine, and chestnut trees.

To identify porcini mushrooms, look for the distinctive caps with spongy undersides and thick, sturdy stems with fine ridges or wrinkles on the top half. They grow individually or in small groups on the forest floor, especially in late summer and fall. Porcini mushrooms are highly sought after by chefs and mushroom enthusiasts for their delicious flavor and culinary versatility. Note that many species in the genus *Boletus* resemble porcinis to some degree, some of which are poisonous. Avoid any bolete with red cap or stem, or with flesh that turns blue when bruised, and always consult an experienced forager before consuming wild mushrooms.

### Matsutake *(Tricholoma magnivelare)*

Matsutake mushrooms are a prized delicacy in Japanese cuisine, known for their spicy aroma and earthy flavor.[58]

Matsutake mushrooms are a prized delicacy in Japanese cuisine, known for their spicy aroma and earthy flavor. These mushrooms have a distinctive white to light brown cap with thick, fibrous scales and a strong, spicy scent reminiscent of cinnamon or pine. Matsutake mushrooms are typically found in mixed woodlands and coniferous forests, especially under pine, fir, and hemlock trees.

To identify matsutake mushrooms, look for their distinctive cap with thick, fibrous scales and a strong, spicy scent. Matsutake mushrooms are highly valued for their unique flavor and aroma, making them a prized find for mushroom foragers and chefs.

### Lobster Mushroom *(Hypomyces lactifluorum)*

Lobster mushrooms can appear in a variety of habitats, depending on the host mushroom.[59]

Lobster mushrooms are a unique and flavorful variety prized for their vibrant color and seafood-like flavor. These mushrooms are parasitic fungi that grow on other mushrooms, typically russula or Lactarius species. Lobster mushrooms have a bright orange-to-red color and a firm, meaty texture. They're normally found in mixed woodlands and coniferous forests, especially under oak, pine, and hemlock trees.

To identify lobster mushrooms, look for their vibrant orange-to-red color, which is produced by the parasite and literally skin deep: like real lobsters, the flesh within should be white, with firm and meaty texture.

Always exercise caution and mindfulness while foraging, especially when distinguishing between edible, inedible, and poisonous species. Take time to familiarize yourself with the key features and habitat preferences of the mushroom varieties. Never consume a mushroom unless you're positive about its identity. When in doubt, err on the side of caution and seek guidance from experienced foragers or mycologists.

# Chapter 6: Cooking Wild Edibles: 15 Easy Recipes

Are you wondering what to do with those wonderful edibles you forage? This chapter includes recipes for all categories, as well as helpful cooking tips for using your bounty safely and efficiently.

All those wonderful edibles you forage can help you create amazing dishes.[60]

# Cooking Tips for Wild Edibles

Before diving into the recipes, familiarize yourself with a few cooking considerations:

- Clean the edibles after gathering them — if you're using them right away, wash them with clean water to remove the soil, small rocks, and animals.

- When working with unfamiliar plants, taste them before trying them in a recipe. You'll only know how to combine them if you know their full flavor profile, texture, etc. Depending on their textures, you can determine the best cooking method.

- Keep in mind that some wild edibles require blanching to another cooking method to remove their bitterness.

- Do you want to highlight your edibles' authentic wild flavor? Find recipes that won't drown out their taste.

- Aren't sure how to incorporate wild edibles into your diet? Why not try adding them to your regular dishes? They can be great substitutes for domesticated variants.

- Add only one or two wild edibles into your recipes until you're familiar with their flavors and how to combine them. You'll fully appreciate their unique taste without overwhelming your dishes.

- If you find some edibles too bitter, combine them with ingredients to balance and improve the flavor profile of the entire dish.

- Some edibles can be prepared in several ways. Experiment with cooking methods to see which brings out their taste the best.

- If you have leftovers you can use within a short period, preserve them for future use. Look into the best preservation for each group and decide based on your preferences. It's one of the best ways to enjoy foraged goods beyond their season.

- If you're out of ideas on how to prepare your goods, reach out to foraging communities for advice. You can exchange tips, recipes, and more.

- Keep a journal of the edibles and recipes you try as a future reference for what works and what doesn't.

# Dandelion Salad

Dandelion greens are packed with vitamins and minerals and can be an excellent twist on your regular salad recipe.[61]

Dandelion greens are packed with vitamins and minerals and can be an excellent twist on your regular salad recipe. You only need the right ingredients to balance the bitterness — as in the recipe described below.

**Ingredients:**

- 1 bunch of dandelion greens (approx. one large handful)
- 1/3 cup of dandelion flowers
- 1 cup of extra virgin olive oil
- 1 pinch of black pepper
- 1 pinch of salt
- ½ cup of orange juice freshly squeezed
- 1 tablespoon of honey (preferably raw, for the full earth taste)
- 2 tablespoons of apple cider vinegar
- 1 cup of butter lettuce
- 1 cup of sugar snap peas
- 1 cucumber (sliced)
- 2 tablespoons of arugula sprouts (optional)

**Instructions:**

1. Combine honey, olive oil, apple cider vinegar, orange juice, salt, and pepper to make the dressing.
2. Chop the lettuce and the dandelion greens. Add them to your favorite salad bowl.
3. Add the sliced cucumber, arugula sprouts, sugar snap peas, and dandelion flowers.
4. Pour the dressing on the top and mix the salad.
5. You can switch the ingredients depending on their seasonal availability. For example, asparagus, green beans, carrots, and radishes pair well with dandelion greens.

# Elderflower Fritters

The following dish is an excellent way to capture elderflowers' endearing sweetness and unique flavor profile. It's a 2-in-1 recipe as it includes making elderflower syrup.

### Ingredients for the elderflower syrup:

- 25 elderflower heads (or about 2 cups of flowers) with stems removed
- 4 cups of water
- Zest of 2 lemons
- Juice of 2 lemons
- 4 cups of sugar
- 1 teaspoon citric acid (optional)

**Instructions:**

1. Remove the flower stalks and place the flowers into a large bowl. Remember, the stems are toxic, so make sure to remove them all.
2. Add the citric acid to the bowl, followed by the lemon zest and juice.
3. Bring the water and sugar to boil in a small saucepan, stirring occasionally.
4. Remove the syrup from the heat once it's boiling, and let it cool down (at room temperature) so it won't burn your fingertips.

5.Pour the cooled syrup into the bowl with the flower and lemon mixture.

6.After stirring to combine, cover the bowl and let it rest for two or three days.

7.Strain the mixture through a fine-meshed sieve lined with a paper towel or cheesecloth into a clean jar.

8.Store the jar in the fridge until further use.

**Ingredients for the fritters:**

- 1 cup of elderflowers
- 2 eggs (beaten)
- 1/2 cup of buttermilk
- 1 1/4 teaspoons of baking powder
- 1/4 cup of sparkling wine (alternatively, you can use beer)
- 2 tablespoons of elderflower cordial
- 1/2 cup of sugar
- 1 pinch of salt
- 1 3/4 cup cake flour or all-purpose flour
- Vegetable oil for frying

**Instructions:**

1.Pour oil into a large, deep pot or a deep fryer. Depending on how deep your oil is, your fritters can be flatter or rounder. If you want larger, rounder fritters, the oil in the pot should be around 4 inches deep.

2.Bring the oil to 350°F on medium heat.

3.Once the oil is almost heated, combine the other ingredients in a separate bowl. Mix until smooth without lumps. Your mixture should be slightly thicker than pancake batter – but not so firm to hold its shape. If it's too thick, add more beer or wine. If it's too thin, stir in a little more flour.

4.Scoop out a tablespoon of fritter batter and drop it into the hot oil. Repeat until you've enough fritters in the oil without overcrowding them (they will stick together and won't fry nicely if there are too many). Work in batches.

5. After 30 seconds, the fritters should float to the surface. If they don't, they might be stuck to the bottom. Dislodge them and fry for 5 minutes or until they become golden brown on both sides.

6. Drain your finished fritters on a paper towel and let them cool.

7. After dusting with a hint of confectioner sugar (optional but can further bring out the sweetness), the fritters will be ready to eat.

8. Serve with the elderflower syrup.

## Blackberry Overnight Oats

This recipe uses many for a nutritious and delicious dessert-for-breakfast experience.[63]

If you've recently foraged a large number of blackberries and don't know what to do with them, this recipe has you covered. It uses many for a nutritious and delicious dessert-for-breakfast experience.

**Ingredients:**

- 1/2 cup of rolled oats
- 2 tablespoons of brown sugar
- 2 teaspoons of chia seeds
- 1/4 cup of plain Greek yogurt or dairy-free yogurt
- 1/2 cup milk of your choice or water
- 1/2 cup of fresh or frozen blackberry
- 1 teaspoon lemon zest (optional)
- Fresh berries (optional for the topping)
- Whipped cream (optional for the topping)

**Instructions:**

1. In a small bowl or jar, combine Greek yogurt, chia seeds, rolled oats, brown sugar, frozen blackberry, lemon zest (if using), and milk.
2. Stir to combine, cover, and place in the fridge. It's best to leave it overnight, but if you want it as a snack, it'll be ready to eat after three to four hours.
3. After staying in the fridge, the oats will absorb most of the liquid. If you prefer your oats thinner, add a little more milk, stir, and it will be ready to eat.
4. Additionally, you can top off your oats with a handful of fresh berries and whipped cream.
5. **The Best Part:** You can make a large batch (by adjusting the ingredients) and keep it in your fridge for up to four days. Perfect for meal prep on busy days.

# Pecan Crusted Chicken

Pecans are the perfect companion to savory, garlicky chicken with their earthy flavor. Here is the recipe for this unique dish:

**Ingredients:**

- 2 large chicken breasts boneless, skinless (around 1 lb.)
- ½ teaspoon of ground black pepper
- 2 teaspoons of sea salt

- 1 tablespoon of plain or gluten-free flour
- 1 cup of pecans crushed
- 1 egg (beaten)
- 1 teaspoon of garlic powder
- ⅓ cup of honey
- 2 tablespoons of olive oil

**Instructions:**

1. Cut the chicken breasts lengthwise and pat them dry before seasoning them with salt and pepper.
2. Chop the pecans into tiny pieces (with a large knife on a cutting board or in the food processor or blender for more uniform pieces).
3. Combine the pecans with garlic powder in a large bowl.
4. In another smaller bowl, beat the eggs. In the meantime, heat the oil in a large skillet.
5. Immerse the chicken into the egg, then into the pecan-garlic mixture. Place them into the skillet.
6. Fry the chicken until it's browned on both sides, which should take four to five minutes per side.
7. Once the chicken is cooked, remove the excess oil and replace it with honey, allowing it to caramelize.
8. After caramelizing, remove the chicken from the skillet and garnish with parsley.

# Wild Mushroom Risotto

Nothing makes a more elegant yet effortless dinner than this wild mushroom risotto recipe with creamy arborio rice and lots of complimentary ingredients.[68]

Nothing makes a more elegant yet effortless dinner than this wild mushroom risotto recipe with creamy arborio rice and lots of complimentary ingredients.

### Ingredients:

- 1 pound (can be a little less) mixed wild mushrooms
- 4 tablespoons of extra-virgin olive oil
- 1 1/2 cups of arborio rice
- 3 large cloves of garlic, peeled and minced
- 2 large shallots, peeled and diced small (about 1/2 cup. You can substitute with yellow onion)
- 1 teaspoon of fresh thyme leaves (plus a little more for garnish)
- 3/4 cup of dry white wine
- 2 ½ teaspoons of kosher salt
- 4-5 cups of warm water (alternatively, use unsalted chicken stock or chicken broth)

- 1/2 cup of grated parmesan cheese (and a little more to garnish)
- 12 turns of fresh-cracked black pepper (or to taste if you're using ground pepper)
- 2 tablespoons of butter

**Instructions:**

1. Heat 3 tablespoons of olive oil over medium heat in a large skillet.
2. Toss in the mushrooms and sprinkle in a pinch of salt.
3. Cook for five minutes or until wilted and lightly browned. Lower the heat to medium-low, and after a minute, occasionally stir if they look too brown too quickly. They should only be slightly brown.
4. Meanwhile, heat the water or chicken broth for the risotto. It will prevent the rice from cooling down, which could prolong the cooking process and alter the texture.
5. When browned, remove the mushrooms from the oil and set them aside.
6. Add the remaining oil to the skillet, the garlic, shallots, or onion (depending on what you use), and the rice. Keep stirring until the rice is completely coated with oil.
7. Pour in the wine and continue stirring until the rice absorbs the liquid.
8. Add the water or chicken broth, thyme, and kosher salt when the rice starts to crackle.
9. Continue stirring until the rice absorbs the liquid. Then, add the next cup of liquid. When that's absorbed, add the next until you've added four cups.
10. Once you've added all the liquid and absorbed by the rice, taste the risotto. It should have a slightly loose texture (not as thick to become a solid lump) and a slight softness — almost al dente.
11. If the risotto is too thick, add a little warm water (up to an additional cup) until you achieve the perfect consistency.
12. When satisfied with the consistency, remove it from the heat and combine it with butter, mushrooms, pepper, and parmesan cheese.

13. Take out the thyme sprig and taste it to see if it needs additional seasoning (depending on your preferences, you may want to add a dash of kosher salt).

14. Serve immediately with a bit of freshly grated parmesan on top. You can store the leftovers in the fridge for two days. If you want to reheat it, add a little warm water to help it regain the primary, porridge-like consistency.

# Chickweed Pesto Pasta

Besides your favorite pasta, you can enjoy this uniquely flavored pesto on crackers as a snack.

### Ingredients:

- A few good handfuls of chickweed tops
- 1–2 cloves of garlic (minced)
- A handful of pine nuts or sunflower seeds
- 1 tablespoon of nutritional yeast (you can substitute it with parmesan cheese)
- A pinch of salt (or to taste)
- 2-3 tablespoons of olive oil

### Instructions:

1. Toss all the ingredients into a blender and blend until it reaches the desired pesto-like consistency and texture.

2. Drizzle in olive oil as needed to ease the blending process. Alternatively, use water if you prefer less oil but want a thinner consistency.

3. When your pesto is ready, combine it with freshly cooked pasta, serve, and enjoy.

# Jerusalem Artichoke Soup

This Jerusalem Artichoke soup is straightforward to make and showcases this veggie's mouthwatering, nutty flavor, with further depth added by the potatoes and onions.

This Jerusalem Artichoke soup is straightforward to make and showcases this veggie's mouthwatering, nutty flavor, with further depth added by the potatoes and onions."

## Ingredients:

- 2 tablespoons of vegetable oil or 3 1/2 tablespoons of butter
- 2 pounds of Jerusalem artichokes
- 1 large onion
- Salt and pepper to taste
- 2 large potatoes
- 4 cups of vegetable stock

## Instructions:

1. Heat the oil or butter in a large casserole or saucepan.
2. In the meantime, peel and cut the Jerusalem artichokes and onion into large chunks. When the oil or butter is heated, toss in the veggies.
3. Season with salt and pepper and fry on medium-low heat until the Jerusalem artichokes soften and the onions become translucent.
4. Toss in the peeled and chopped potatoes.

5. Pour in the veggie stock and bring to a boil.

6. After cooking the soup for 20 minutes, remove it from the heat and allow to cool.

7. Transfer it to a food processor and blend until smooth. Alternatively, you can use an immersion blender to blend. Add a little warm water to reach the perfect cream soup consistency if necessary.

# Fried Chicken of the Woods Sandwich

Did you know that Chicken of the Woods can taste like fried chicken? Try this recipe and find out. You only need your favorite indulging-worthy toppings like lettuce, ranch, pickles, etc., and you'll have the perfect Southeast fried dinner.

**Ingredients:**

- 16 ounces of chicken of the woods
- 2 cups of flour
- 7 large eggs
- 1 teaspoon of mace
- 2 teaspoons of sea salt
- Olive oil, enough to coat
- 1/2 teaspoon of black pepper
- 1 teaspoon of allspice
- 1 teaspoon of thyme
- 1 teaspoon of sage
- 1 teaspoon of dill
- 1 teaspoon of oregano
- 1 teaspoon of onion powder
- 1 teaspoon of garlic powder
- 4 onion buns
- Lettuce, as needed
- Tomato, sliced, as needed
- Butter pickles, as needed
- Ranch, or another dressing of your choice

## Instructions:

1. Beat the eggs in a bowl. In another bowl, combine all the seasoning with the flour.

2. Dip the Chicken from the Woods into the egg, then into the seasoned flour mixture.

3. Once it's fully coated, spray a little oil on it.

4. Cook in a preheated oven or air fryer at 270 degrees for 20 minutes (flipping after 10).

5. When cooked, place your Chicken of the Woods on a bun and dress it up with your favorite toppings. (Use the ones suggested in the ingredient list, or go for your own. The choice is yours).

# Sumac Shoot Salad

Sumac shoots have a fruity and tart flavor, making them an excellent flavor enhancer in salads.

## Ingredients:

- 2 cups of sumac roots, chopped and a little dried
- 2 cups of diced tomatoes
- ½ cup of diced red onion
- 2 cups of diced cucumbers
- ½ cup of fresh parsley, finely chopped and stems removed
- ½ cup of olive oil
- ¼ cup of fresh lemon juice
- 2 teaspoons of kosher salt
- ¼ cup of distilled white vinegar
- 1 tablespoon of pomegranate molasses, optional

Sumac shoots have a fruity and tart flavor, making them an excellent flavor enhancer in salads.[65]

**Instructions:**

1. Mix vinegar, lemon juice, salt, oil, and pomegranate molasses in a small bowl.

2. Combine the sumac, parsley, onions, cucumbers, and tomatoes in a larger bowl.

3. Pour the dressing over the vegetables and gently mix until evenly coated.

---

# Steamed Wood Nettle Shoots

Wood nettle can be the perfect substitute for spinach as a side. It has a slightly deeper flavor, which goes well with dishes that complement its strengths.

**Ingredients:**

- 2 tablespoons of extra virgin olive oil or melted butter for serving
- 8 ounces of fresh wood nettle shoots
- Kosher salt or flaky finishing salt to taste for serving

**Instructions:**

1. Pour a few inches of water into a deep steamer pot and bring it to a boil on high heat.

2. Place in the steamer basket, followed by the wood nettle shots.

3. Cover the pot and bring the water to boil on medium-high.

4. Cook for five minutes, then taste the shoots. They should be tender and green but slightly crunchy. The longer you cook them, the more intense their taste will become. Five minutes of cooking will be enough if you don't want them to overpower your main dish (you don't want to turn them into mush).

5. Serve the shoots with salt and oil to the side so everyone can season to their liking.

# Black Locust Flower Jelly

Here is how to turn black locust flowers into a mouthwatering jelly, reminding you of peach preserves. First, make black locust flower tea.

### Ingredients for the Tea:

- 2 cups of black locust flowers, stems removed

- 3 cups of water

### Instructions:

1. Put the black locust flowers into a heat-safe container (this is crucial as you'll be streaming hot water over them) and set them aside.

Here is how to turn black locust flowers into a mouthwatering jelly, reminding you of peach preserves.[66]

2. Bring water to a boil in a pot.

3. Once ready, pour the boiling water onto the flowers. Give them a stir so every flower is submerged in the water.

4. Clover the container (loosely to let some of the condensation out) and set it aside.

5. Steep it for 12-24 hours, depending on how strong you want your tea. If steeping for an entire day, let it cool to room temperature, then put it in the fridge for the remaining time (otherwise, it can spoil, especially if the temperatures are high).

6. After 12-24 hours, strain the liquid over gauze or a fine mesh sieve. Press the flowers to squeeze all the liquid out before discarding them. The more liquid you have, the more jelly you can make in the subsequent process. You should have 2 1/2 -2

3/4 cups of pale yellow colored (or pale tan, depending on strength) tea.

7. You can use the back locust tea to make jelly right away or freeze it for later use. You can store it frozen for up to three months.

## Ingredients for the Jelly:

- 2 1/2 cups of black locust flower tea
- 2 tablespoons of lemon juice
- 1 pack of Jello or no-sugar powdered pectin
- 2 1/2 cups of sugar
- 1/2 teaspoon butter (to reduce foaming, add it at any point during cooking)

## Instructions:

1. Pour the tea into a large pot (it should be large enough to account for heavy foaming and a bit of splashing when boiling). If you're using frozen tea, thaw it out beforehand. You can leave it out at room temperature overnight or drop it into the pot and let it liquefy over low heat.

2. When the tea is ready (thawed or prepared), add the lemon juice and stir.

3. As it warms up, the liquid will clear but will go back to yellow or tannish (depending on how strong you made your tea in the previous step) later.

4. Pour 2 1/2 cups of sugar into a large bowl, take 1/4 of a cup's worth into a smaller bowl, then set the larger bowl aside.

5. Combine the sugar with a packet of powdered pectin in the smaller bowl.

6. Add the mixture from the previous step to the warming tea and lemon juice concoction.

7. Turn the heat to high and bring to boil, stirring constantly to avoid burning.

8. Once the mixture comes to a boil, stir in the sugar from the larger bowl you set aside.

9. You'll notice the mixture stops boiling as soon as you add the sugar. It will soon return to boiling point, so be careful when taking the next step.

10. After boiling for one minute and stirring vigorously, add the butter to reduce foaming. Do it slowly to avoid splashing and burning yourself with the boiling liquid.

11. After a minute, remove the jelly from the heat. You'll notice it starts setting immediately, so you must quickly transfer it into the prepared jars (don't rush so you burn yourself, but don't let the jelly set in the pot either).

12. If you're canning the jelly, leave a 1/4 inch headspace at the jar tops, and remove the bubbles forming on the surface. Clean the rims to ensure the jars can be sealed properly.

13. If you aren't canning it, let it sit in the jars for 12-24 hours or until it cools to room temperature. Transfer the jars to the fridge and store them for three weeks. Ensure you clean the jars from jelly residue on the outside before storing them.

14. Alternatively, you can freeze it. In this way, it will keep for several months.

# Persimmons Bread

Persimmons taste similar to sweet pumpkins and apples but can be an excellent substitute for bananas. If you like making banana bread, you'll love this recipe.

**Ingredients:**

- 3 cups pureed persimmon
- 2 large eggs, room temperature
- 1 cup of granulated sugar
- 1 tablespoon of vanilla extract
- 10 tablespoons of unsalted butter, melted
- 2 teaspoons of cinnamon
- 2 teaspoons of baking soda
- 1/4 teaspoon of salt
- 1 cup of raisins
- 3 cups of all-purpose flour
- 1 1/2 cups of walnut pieces, toasted

**Instructions:**

1. Preheat the oven to 350°F and prepare two bread loaf pans by coating them with butter.

2. Toast the walnuts in a dry skillet until they acquire a light golden color and a stronger aroma.

3. Cut the persimmons tops with a sturdy knife, chop the remaining part into quarters, then toss into the blender to puree. In the meantime, melt the butter.

4. Whisk the eggs, sugar, and vanilla extract in a large bowl. Combine with the melted butter and the persimmon puree.

5. Add the salt, baking soda, and cinnamon, stir, then add the flour. Stir until everything is combined into a uniform texture.

6. Gently fold in the raisins and the walnuts, then pour the batter equally into the two loaf pans.

7. Bake for 45 minutes or until done (do the well-tried toothpick check to verify).

8. After cooling them in the pans for 10 minutes, transfer your loaves onto a wire rack to cool completely at room temperature.

# Mullein Syrup

Mullein syrup is one of the best natural medicines for respiratory ailments.

**Ingredients:**

- 1 ½ cups of water
- 1-2 teaspoons of dried mullein flowers or leaves or a combination of both
- 1-2 teaspoons of honey – you may need more if you want your syrup to be thick and sweet

**Instructions:**

1. Bring the water to a boil, then add the dried mullein flowers or leaves.

2. Let the water boil for 5 minutes before removing it from the stove. Allow it to cool at room temperature.

3. After a couple of hours, the concoction will be ready to strain. Use gauze or a cheesecloth to transfer it into a glass or plastic container.

4. Press down the leaves and flowers to get all the water (and aroma) out. When no more water is dripping through the gauze, discard the plant material.

5. Add honey to the liquid while stirring. Let the honey thicken to your desired consistency.

6. Store the syrup in the fridge for up to 30 days and use as needed.

# Aromatic Yarrow Tea

Enjoy a cup of earth tea as a reward for your foraging efforts.[67]

Enjoy a cup of earth tea as a reward for your foraging efforts.

### Ingredients:

- 1 teaspoon of dried yarrow
- 1 cup of boiling water
- Sugar or sweetener, to taste

### Instructions:

1. Add boiling water to the dried yarrow leaf and steep it for approximately 10 minutes.

2. Strain and sweeten to taste, as it can taste somewhat bitter. It's recommended to use a natural sweetener.

3. Drink the tea before going to sleep to relax and ease pain flare-ups.

# Red Clover Tea

This tea will help you combine the useful with the purposeful. Relax while drinking it. It will heal you from the inside out.

**Ingredients:**

- 1 tablespoon of dried red clover flower
- 1 cup of water
- Sweetener to taste (optional)

**Instructions:**

1. Pour a cup of boiling water on the dried flowers, then steep for 10 minutes.
2. Consume tea up to 4 times a day for stomach issues, colds, and infections.
3. Sweeten if you prefer, but it will work more efficiently against infections if you don't add sugar (you can use other non-sugar-based sweeteners).

# Chapter 7: Medicinal Plants of the Southeast

Did you know that some of the most effective remedies for common illnesses may be growing right in your backyard? The use of plants for healing is a practice dating back thousands of years. The tradition of using medicinal plants has been used for countless generations, from the ancient Egyptians and Chinese to Native American tribes. How else would people treat illnesses before the advent of modern pharmaceuticals? They turned to nature. Plants like Echinacea and Goldenseal have been used for centuries to boost immunity and fight infections. If you've ever sipped chamomile tea to soothe a sore throat or calm your nerves, you know how effective medicinal plants can be.

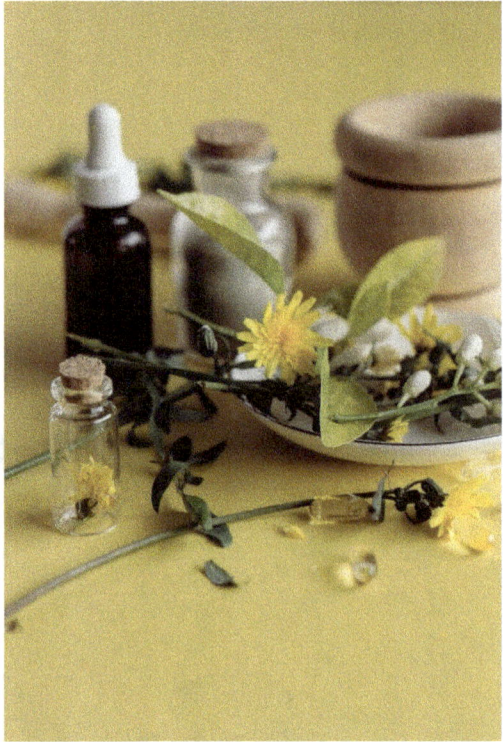

The tradition of using medicinal plants is about a holistic approach to health.[68]

The tradition of using medicinal plants is not only about treating symptoms. It's about a holistic approach to health. Have you considered the overall wellness benefits of incorporating natural remedies into your daily routine? You can combine these plants to create effective natural medicines. Moreover, suppose you've ever felt overwhelmed by the side effects of synthetic drugs. In that case, you may find solace in knowing that many people turn to plants for many illnesses, including mental health. These plants offer therapeutic benefits with fewer side effects, making them a gentle yet effective alternative.

Have you ever tried making herbal remedies? It's easier than you think. Simple preparations like teas, tinctures, and salves can be made at home with only a few ingredients. There's something deeply satisfying about harvesting your own medicine and using it to improve your health. So, whether you're new to herbalism or looking to deepen your understanding, exploring the world of medicinal plants offers a rewarding journey into natural health and wellness. The Southeast is rich with plants that have been used for centuries for healing.

# Disclaimers and Safety Precautions

Using medicinal plants can be a wonderful way to enhance your health. However, approaching them with caution and respect is crucial. Did you know even natural remedies can cause serious health issues if not used correctly? Here are some essential safety precautions to keep in mind to ensure you use these powerful plants safely and effectively.

### Consult Healthcare Providers

Firstly, it's always important to consult your healthcare provider before using any medicinal plants, especially if you have existing health conditions or are taking other medications. Have you ever considered how plants may interact with your prescriptions? For instance, St. John's Wort, which is frequently used to treat depression, may have unexpected effects by decreasing the efficacy of birth control pills and other drugs.

Consider the case of John, who decided to use Goldenseal to help with a persistent cold. Without consulting his doctor, he didn't realize that Goldenseal can increase blood pressure. John already had high blood pressure, and after taking Goldenseal, his condition worsened, leading to a medical emergency.

Do you ever think about the exact dosage when you take herbal supplements? Unlike prescription drugs, the dosage of medicinal plants can be tricky to determine. For instance, Echinacea is great for boosting immunity, but taking too much can cause nausea, dizziness, and allergic reactions. If you've ever experienced an allergic reaction, you know how scary it can be.

### Proper Identification

If you plan to forage medicinal plants, proper identification is crucial. Mistaking one plant for another can have dangerous consequences. For example, someone once mistakenly identified a plant they thought was Wild Yam, which is beneficial for hormonal balance, but it was a toxic look-alike. This resulted in severe gastrointestinal distress and a trip to the emergency room.

### Preparation Methods

Have you ever made herbal tea? It's a simple and effective way to use medicinal plants, but preparation methods matter. Using too much plant material or the wrong part of the plant can lead to adverse effects. For example, parts of the Elderberry plant are toxic if not properly prepared. Consuming uncooked Elderberries or the bark and leaves can cause nausea, vomiting, and diarrhea.

### General Safety Considerations

Think about your allergies. Even if you're not allergic to a plant, the way it's prepared could introduce allergens. For instance, a person with a ragweed allergy may react to Echinacea because the plants are related. Always test a small amount first if you're trying a new herb.

If you've ever thought about making herbal remedies, always start with small doses and see how your body reacts. Remember, more isn't always better. A small dose of a tincture might be therapeutic, but too much could cause harm. For instance, Lobelia is useful for respiratory issues but can be toxic in high doses, leading to nausea, sweating, and, in severe cases, death.

Finally, always be mindful of your body's responses. Have you ever felt off after trying something new? Listen to those signals. If you experience adverse reactions, stop using the plant immediately and seek medical advice. For example, if you use Black Cohosh for menopausal symptoms and experience stomach discomfort or unusual bleeding, consult your doctor.

# Plant Profiles

## Echinacea *(Echinacea purpurea)*

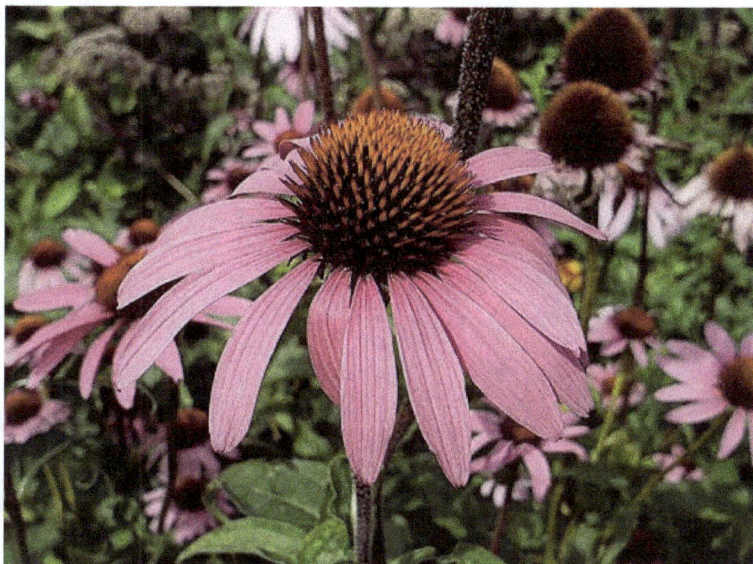

Echinacea, known as coneflower, is a popular medicinal plant known for its immune-boosting properties.[69]

Echinacea, known as coneflower, is a popular medicinal plant known for its immune-boosting properties. Echinacea is well-known for helping to reduce the severity and duration of colds and flu. It stimulates the immune system, making it more effective at fighting off infections.

If you're feeling under the weather, you can make a simple Echinacea tea by steeping the dried roots or leaves in hot water for about 10-15 minutes. Drinking this tea a few times a day at the first sign of symptoms can help your body fend off illness more effectively. Gargling with Echinacea tea can soothe a sore throat and reduce inflammation. Brew a strong cup of tea, let it cool a bit, and gargle for a few minutes before swallowing.

## American Ginseng *(Panax quinquefolius)*

American Ginseng is a powerful herb known for its adaptogenic properties, meaning it helps the body adapt to stress and boosts overall energy and vitality. One of the primary benefits of American Ginseng is its ability to enhance physical and mental performance. Consider taking American Ginseng in capsule or tincture form to improve focus and stamina.

Do you ever have those days where you can't shake the fatigue? Drinking American Ginseng tea can help. To make the tea, steep about a teaspoon of dried, chopped ginseng root in hot water for 10-15 minutes. Drinking this tea once or twice a day can provide a natural boost without the jitters that often come with caffeine.

## Goldenseal *(Hydrastis canadensis)*

Goldenseal is a versatile medicinal plant known for its antimicrobial and anti-inflammatory properties.[70]

Goldenseal is a versatile medicinal plant known for its antimicrobial and anti-inflammatory properties. One of the primary uses of Goldenseal is treating respiratory infections and colds. You can take Goldenseal in capsule or tincture form at the first sign of a cold. A few drops of Goldenseal tincture in water, taken a few times a day, can help shorten the duration of your symptoms.

Goldenseal is known for its digestive health benefits. If you experience digestive discomfort, such as bloating or indigestion, Goldenseal could help. It stimulates the production of digestive enzymes and bile, improving digestion and alleviating symptoms.

For those suffering from sinus infections, Goldenseal can provide relief. A saline nasal rinse with a few drops of Goldenseal tincture can help clear the sinuses and reduce inflammation. If you've ever had a sinus infection, you know how miserable it can be. This natural remedy might offer much-needed relief.

## Passionflower *(Passiflora incarnata)*

Passionflower is a beautiful and potent medicinal plant known for its calming effects and ability to treat various ailments, particularly those relating to the nervous system. It is a natural remedy for anxiety and stress. To make passionflower tea, steep a teaspoon of dried Passionflower in boiled water for about 10-15 minutes. Drinking this tea in the evening can help you unwind and improve sleep quality.

If you've ever struggled with insomnia, Passionflower can be particularly helpful. Instead of reaching for over-the-counter sleep aids, consider taking Passionflower in capsule or tincture form. A few drops of Passionflower tincture in water or juice before bed can help you fall asleep faster and enjoy a more restful night.

## Black Cohosh *(Actaea racemosa)*

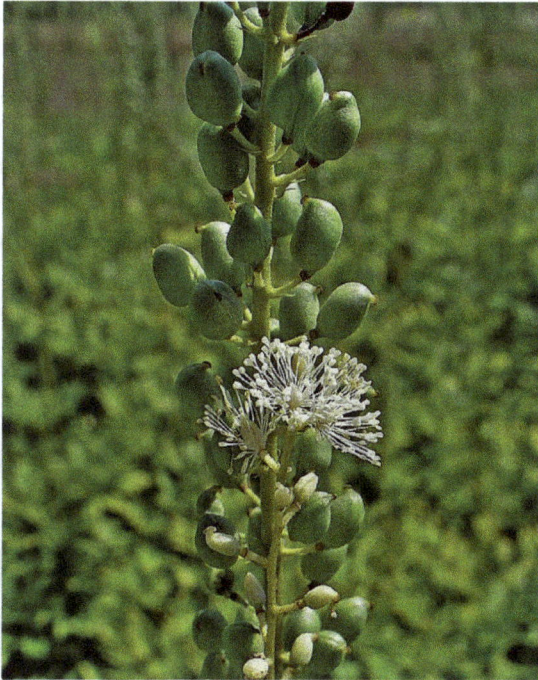

Black Cohosh is a well-known medicinal plant primarily used for women's health, especially in managing menopause symptoms and menstrual discomfort.[7]

Black Cohosh is a well-known medicinal plant primarily used for women's health, especially in managing menopause symptoms and menstrual discomfort. If you've ever been woken up by night sweats, you know how disruptive it can be. Taking Black Cohosh in capsule or tincture form can help balance your hormones and reduce these uncomfortable symptoms. Typically, a standard dose is around 20-40 mg of standardized extract, taken once or twice daily.

For menstrual discomfort, Black Cohosh can be a lifesaver. Have you ever had debilitating menstrual cramps or PMS? Drinking Black Cohosh tea or taking it in supplement form can help alleviate cramping and mood-related symptoms. To make tea with this plant, steep a teaspoon of dried Black Cohosh root in hot water for 10-15 minutes. Drink this a few times a day during your menstrual cycle for relief.

### Elderberry *(Sambucus* spp.*)*

Elderberry is a powerful plant well-known for its immune-boosting and antiviral properties. You know how important it is to act quickly to the onset of a cold. Elderberry syrup, taken at the first sign of symptoms, can help shorten the duration of a cold and reduce the severity of symptoms. You can make your syrup by simmering dried elderberries with water, honey, and a bit of cinnamon and cloves for added flavor and benefits.

Elderberry is available in other forms, such as lozenges, gummies, and capsules. If you prefer a quick and convenient option, elderberry gummies or capsules taken daily during the cold season can provide a consistent immune boost.

While Elderberry is generally safe for most people, it's important to prepare it properly. Raw elderberries, the bark, leaves, and seeds, contain compounds that can cause nausea and vomiting. Always cook elderberries before consuming them.

### Boneset *(Eupatorium perfoliatum)*

Boneset is a medicinal plant known for its effectiveness in treating fever and flu symptoms.[73]

Boneset is a medicinal plant known for its effectiveness in treating fever and flu symptoms. Drinking Boneset tea can help lower your fever and ease body aches. To make tea with it, steep a teaspoon of dried Boneset leaves in boiled water for 10-15 minutes. Drink this tea a few times a day while experiencing symptoms. Boneset helps break up congestion and clear the respiratory tract.

Boneset has anti-inflammatory properties. Have you ever dealt with inflammation from an injury or chronic condition? Applying a cooled Boneset tea or tincture compress to the affected area can help reduce inflammation and promote healing.

### Wild Yam (Dioscorea villosa)

Wild Yam is commonly used to alleviate menstrual cramps and premenstrual syndrome (PMS). Drinking Wild Yam tea or taking it in capsule form can help soothe cramps. To make tea using Wild Yam, steep a teaspoon of dried root in boiled water for about 10-15 minutes. Drinking this tea a few times a day during your menstrual cycle can provide relief.

For menopausal symptoms such as hot flashes and night sweats, Wild Yam can be beneficial. Using a Wild Yam cream or taking it as a supplement can help balance hormones and reduce these symptoms. Apply the cream to your skin as directed, usually once or twice daily, or take the supplement.

Wild Yam is known for its anti-inflammatory properties. Wild Yam might help with joint pain or inflammation. Applying a topical Wild Yam cream to the affected areas can reduce inflammation and provide pain relief.

### Sweet Goldenrod (Solidago odora)

Sweet Goldenrod is a delightful medicinal plant known for its aromatic qualities and various health benefits. Drinking Sweet Goldenrod tea can help indigestion or bloating. To make this tea, steep a teaspoon of dried Sweet Goldenrod leaves in hot water for 10-15 minutes. Drinking this tea after meals can aid digestion and reduce bloating.

For those with allergies, Sweet Goldenrod can provide relief. Have you ever suffered from seasonal allergies and sought natural remedies? Sweet Goldenrod tea or tincture can help reduce allergy symptoms, such as sneezing and runny nose.

## Saw Palmetto *(Serenoa repens)*

One of the primary benefits of Saw Palmetto is supporting prostate health.[78]

One of the primary benefits of Saw Palmetto is supporting prostate health. If you have concerns about prostate enlargement or benign prostatic hyperplasia (BPH), Saw Palmetto might be a natural remedy worth considering. For men dealing with hair loss, Saw Palmetto could be beneficial. Have you noticed thinning hair or bald patches? Saw Palmetto blocks the conversion of testosterone to dihydrotestosterone (DHT), a hormone linked to hair loss. Incorporating Saw Palmetto supplements into your daily routine might help slow down hair loss and promote hair regrowth.

Additionally, Saw Palmetto has been used traditionally to boost libido and sexual function in men. Do you feel a decline in your sexual desire or performance? Saw Palmetto may help improve libido and erectile function by balancing hormone levels and promoting overall prostate health.

## Red Clover *(Trifolium pratense)*

Red Clover is beneficial for bone health. Are you worried about osteoporosis or bone density loss? Red Clover contains compounds called isoflavones, which have been shown to support bone health and reduce the risk of osteoporosis. Incorporating Red Clover supplements into your daily routine, with regular exercise and a healthy diet, can help maintain strong and healthy bones as you age.

Red Clover is also known for its detoxifying properties. Do you feel the need to cleanse your body and rid it of toxins? Red Clover tea can support liver health and promote detoxification, helping your body eliminate waste and toxins more efficiently.

**Yarrow** *(Achillea millefolium)*

One of the primary uses of Yarrow is in wound healing.[74]

One of the primary uses of Yarrow is in wound healing. Applying a poultice or salve from Yarrow leaves can help stop bleeding and promote faster healing from a minor cut or scrape. Yarrow contains compounds with antimicrobial and anti-inflammatory properties, making it an effective natural remedy for minor wounds and skin irritations.

Additionally, Yarrow is known for its immune-boosting properties. Do you feel run down and in need of an immune boost? Regularly drinking Yarrow tea can support your immune system and help your body fight off infections more effectively. Yarrow contains compounds with antimicrobial properties, making it a valuable ally in maintaining overall health and wellness.

### St. John's Wort *(Hypericum perforatum)*

St. John's Wort is a well-known medicinal plant used primarily for its mood-enhancing properties and to alleviate symptoms of depression and anxiety. Have you struggled with low mood or felt overwhelmed by stress? St. John's Wort may be the natural remedy you need to lift your spirits. St. John's Wort increases serotonin levels, a neurotransmitter that plays a key role in regulating mood.

For those with anxiety or nervousness, St. John's Wort can offer relief. Suppose you feel on edge or struggle with racing thoughts. In that case, St. John's Wort has calming properties to help reduce anxiety and promote relaxation. Drinking St. John's Wort tea or taking it as a supplement can help soothe frazzled nerves and ease tension.

St. John's Wort is beneficial for improving sleep quality. Do you have trouble falling or staying asleep throughout the night? St. John's Wort can help regulate sleep patterns and promote restful sleep. Taking it before bedtime helps calm the mind and prepares you for a peaceful night's rest.

### Wild Indigo *(Baptisia tinctoria)*

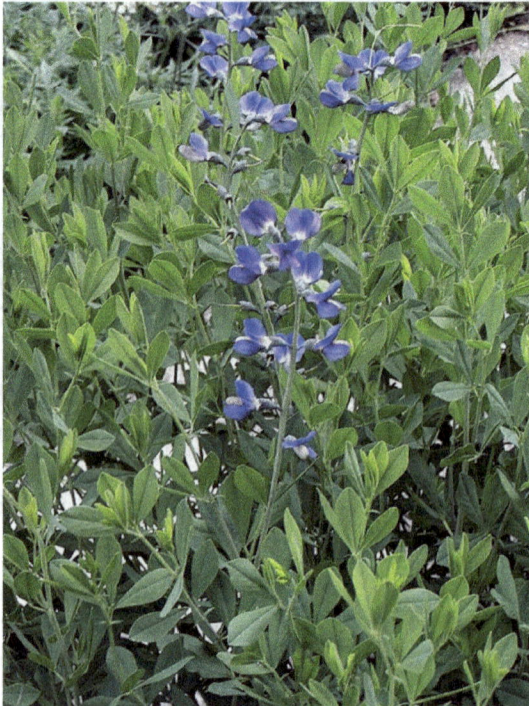

Wild Indigo is a powerful medicinal plant known for its immune-boosting properties and to fight off infections.[75]

Wild Indigo is a powerful medicinal plant known for its immune-boosting properties and to fight off infections. Are you run down and need an immune boost? Wild Indigo might be the natural remedy to support your body's defenses.

One of the primary benefits of Wild Indigo is that it stimulates the immune system. Taking Wild Indigo supplements or drinking it as a tea can help strengthen your immune system and reduce the frequency and severity of infections, like a cold making the rounds. Wild Indigo contains compounds that activate immune cells, making it an effective ally in fighting off viruses and bacteria.

For those with respiratory infections, Wild Indigo can offer relief. Have you had a stubborn cough or congestion that wouldn't go away? Wild Indigo has expectorant properties that loosen mucus and clear the airways. Drinking Wild Indigo tea or using it as a gargle can help soothe a sore throat and ease respiratory symptoms.

Also, Wild Indigo is beneficial for treating skin and mucous membrane infections. If you have a minor cut or a sore throat, applying a Wild Indigo poultice or using it as a mouthwash can help disinfect the area and promote faster healing. Wild Indigo contains antimicrobial compounds that aid in killing bacteria and preventing infection.

### Lobelia *(Lobelia inflata)*

One of the primary uses of Lobelia is treating respiratory conditions, such as asthma, bronchitis, and coughs. Do you have difficulty breathing or experience wheezing during an asthma attack? Lobelia helps relax the airways and improves breathing. Drinking Lobelia tea or using it as a steam inhalation helps reduce inflammation in the lungs and eases respiratory symptoms.

Lobelia is beneficial for alleviating muscle tension and spasms. Lobelia has muscle relaxant properties that relieve tension and promote relaxation for tight muscles and muscle cramps. Applying a Lobelia poultice or using it in a massage oil soothes sore muscles and eases discomfort.

For those with digestive issues, Lobelia can offer relief. Have you had indigestion or experienced nausea? Lobelia can stimulate digestion and relieve nausea by increasing gastric secretions and promoting bile flow.

## Blackberry *(Rubus* spp.*)*

Blackberries are commonly found throughout the southeastern region, thriving in fields, along forest edges, and in disturbed areas.[76]

Blackberries are commonly found throughout the southeastern region, thriving in fields, along forest edges, and in disturbed areas. The leaves and roots are traditionally used to treat diarrhea and inflammation. The berries are rich in vitamins and antioxidants, making them a nutritious addition to diets. When foraging for blackberries, make sure to identify the thorny canes with five-leaflet leaves and white or pink flowers that precede the berries. Be cautious of look-alike plants like raspberry, which have similar fruit but a different leaf structure. Harvest the leaves in spring and the berries in late summer.

### Jewelweed *(Impatiens capensis)*

Jewelweed is found in moist, shady areas, along streams, and wetlands. It's well-known for treating poison ivy, insect bites, and other skin irritations. The plant has distinctive orange, yellow, or red-spotted flowers and succulent stems that release a juice when crushed. To forage jewelweed, look for its teardrop-shaped leaves and touch-me-not seed pods, which explode upon contact. There are no toxic look-alikes, but ensure you forage in a clean area away from pollution.

# Marshmallow *(Althaea officinalis)*

Marshmallows grow in marshy fields, along riverbanks, and in damp meadows."

Marshmallows grow in marshy fields, along riverbanks, and in damp meadows. The roots are used for soothing mucous membranes in the respiratory and digestive systems. The plant features soft, velvety leaves and pale pink to white flowers. When foraging marshmallows, identify them by their height (up to 4 feet) and their hairy stems and leaves. It can be confused with other mallows, but marshmallow's medicinal properties are superior. Harvest the roots in late fall when the plant's energy is concentrated below ground.

## Mullein *(Verbascum thapsus)*

Mullein thrives in dry, sunny locations along roadsides and open fields. The leaves and flowers are used for respiratory conditions like coughs and bronchitis. Mullein is easily identifiable by its tall, single spike of yellow flowers and large, fuzzy leaves. Look out for potential confusion with lamb's ear, which has similar fuzzy leaves but a different flower structure. Harvest mullein leaves when young and flowers are in full bloom, typically from late spring to summer.

## Witch Hazel *(Hamamelis virginiana)*

Witch hazel is found in forests and along streams in the southeastern U.S.[78]

Witch hazel is found in forests and along streams in the southeastern US; its bark and leaves are used for skin conditions, hemorrhoids, and varicose veins. The plant is recognizable by its unique yellow, spidery flowers that bloom in late fall or winter and its smooth, gray bark. When foraging, ensure proper identification to avoid confusion with hazelnut shrubs, which have similar leaves but different flowers and fruit. Harvest the bark and leaves in the fall when the plant is most potent.

# Incorporating Medicinal Plants into Daily Life

## Making Teas

Herbal teas are one of the simplest and most enjoyable ways to benefit from medicinal plants. To make an herbal tea, start by selecting your desired herbs. You can use fresh or dried herbs, depending on availability and preference.

### Steps to Make Herbal Tea

1. Measure the desired herbs (typically 1-2 teaspoons per cup of water).
2. Heat water to just below boiling and pour it over the herbs.

3. Cover and steep for 5-10 minutes or longer for a stronger infusion.

4. Strain and enjoy your herbal tea hot or cold.

**Popular Herbal Tea Blends**

- **Immune Boosting Blend:** Echinacea, elderberry, and ginger.
- **Relaxation Blend:** Chamomile, lemon balm, and lavender.
- **Digestive Aid Blend:** Peppermint, fennel, and ginger.

# Creating Tinctures

Herbal tinctures are concentrated liquid extracts from soaking herbs in alcohol or glycerin. They are convenient for long-term storage and easy to dose.

### Steps to Make Herbal Tinctures

1. Chop or crush the herbs and place them in a clean glass jar.
2. Cover the herbs with alcohol (vodka or brandy) or glycerin.
3. Seal the jar tightly and store it in a cool, dark place for several weeks, shaking it daily.
4. Strain the tincture through cheesecloth or a fine mesh strainer and store it in dark glass bottles.
5. **Dosage:** Typically, 1-2 dropperfuls (about 30-60 drops) diluted in water, juice, or tea, taken 2-3 times per day.

# Making Poultices

Herbal poultices are moist herbal preparations applied externally to the skin to promote healing and relieve inflammation.

### Steps to Make Herbal Poultices

1. Prepare a strong infusion of the desired herbs by steeping them in hot water.
2. Strain the liquid and soak a clean cloth or gauze in the herbal infusion.
3. Apply the soaked cloth directly to the affected area and cover it with a warm towel or bandage.
4. Leave the poultice on for 15-30 minutes, then remove and discard.

**Herbs Used for Poultices:** Plantain for insect bites, comfrey for bruises, and calendula for minor cuts and scrapes.

# Formulating Salves

Herbal salves are semi-solid preparations made by infusing herbs in oil and combining them with beeswax to create a soothing topical ointment.

### Steps to Make Herbal Salves

1. Infuse dried herbs in a carrier oil (like olive or coconut oil) using a double boiler or slow cooker.
2. Strain the infused oil and combine it with melted beeswax at a ratio of approximately 4 parts oil to 1 part beeswax.
3. Transfer the mixture into sterile, clean jars or tins, then let it cool and harden.

**Uses:** Apply salves topically to soothe dry skin, relieve muscle aches, or promote wound healing.

Exploring medicinal plants in the Southeast offers a fascinating journey into the rich tradition of herbalism and natural remedies. From the ancient practices of indigenous cultures to modern holistic health approaches, using plants for healing has endured through the ages.

As you discover new uses for medicinal plants, approaching their use with reverence, responsibility, and respect is imperative. While these plants offer valuable therapeutic benefits, you must recognize the importance of informed consent, consultation with healthcare professionals, and adherence to safety guidelines.

# Chapter 8: The Southeast Forager's Lifestyle

How do you know you want a foraging lifestyle? Maybe you're tired of the same old routine of waking up, going to work, grabbing a quick lunch from the nearest fast-food joint, coming home exhausted, and repeating it all the next day. Maybe you long for something different, something more meaningful and connected. You feel a pull toward nature, a desire to step away from the hustle and bustle and find peace in the simplicity of the natural world.

You feel a pull toward nature, a desire to step away from the hustle and bustle and find peace in the simplicity of the natural world."

Or perhaps you've felt the weight of modern life bearing down on you. The constant noise, the screens, the endless notifications—it all feels overwhelming. Maybe you yearn for the quiet that only nature can offer. This is what foraging is about – reconnecting with nature.

Have you ever thought about the food you eat, where it comes from, how it's grown, and what's in it? Foraging offers a refreshing alternative if you're tired of the endless aisles of processed foods and the lack of connection to what's on your plate. Picture this: instead of picking up a plastic-wrapped vegetable from the supermarket, you step outside and find fresh, wild greens growing in your backyard or local park. The satisfaction of harvesting your food, knowing where it came from and how it was grown, is unparalleled.

Or, maybe you're concerned about your health. You've tried various diets and health trends, but none stick. Foraging introduces you to a whole new world of nutritious, natural foods free from the chemicals and additives in store-bought produce. Wild foods are notably richer in nutrients and offer unique flavors you won't find in conventional foods.

You may be drawn to foraging because of a love for cooking and experimenting in the kitchen. The idea of working with fresh, wild ingredients excites you. Each trip outdoors can become a culinary adventure as you discover new flavors and textures to bring into your kitchen.

In short, a foraging lifestyle can be the answer if you feel a call for a change—a desire to live more naturally, sustainably, and mindfully. It's a journey reconnecting you with nature, nourishing your body, mind, and spirit, and offering fulfillment that modern life lacks. This chapter is about learning to adopt the forager's mindset and lifestyle.

### Cultivating a Forager's Mindset

This mindset involves a deeper appreciation for the natural world and a commitment to lifelong learning. It's about approaching every foraging adventure with observation, curiosity, and respect for the interconnectedness of all living things.

### Observation and Curiosity

The first step in cultivating a forager's mindset is learning to observe and be curious about your surroundings. When out in nature, take time to notice the details. Look at the different plants, the textures of their leaves, the colors of their flowers, and the habitats they thrive in. For example, in the Southeast, you might come across the lush greenery of chickweed in shaded, moist areas or the vibrant blooms of red clover in open fields.

Start a nature journal. Take notes and sketch the plants you see every time you go foraging – and record where you found them, the time of year, and other details that stand out. Over time, this journal will become a valuable resource, helping you track seasonal changes and plant behaviors.

### Respect for Nature's Interconnectedness

A key aspect of the forager's mindset is respecting the interconnectedness of all living things. When you forage, you must do so sustainably and ensure you don't harm the environment or deplete resources. For example, when harvesting ramps (wild leeks), a popular foraged item in the Southeast, take only one or two leaves from each plant instead of uprooting the entire plant. This way, the ramps can continue to grow and reproduce, supporting the ecosystem and future foragers.

Follow the "rule of thirds." When you find a patch of edible plants, take only one-third, leaving the rest to continue growing and supporting the ecosystem. This approach ensures that the plants can regenerate and that the wildlife relying on them also has enough to eat.

### Deepening Knowledge Through Learning

Learning to forage is a lifetime process. There's always something new to learn, be it a new use for a common wild food or a plant you've never seen before. Take advantage of the many resources available to deepen your knowledge.

Join local foraging groups or attend workshops. In the Southeast, organizations like the Georgia Botanical Society or the Florida Native Plant Society often host educational events and foraging walks. These gatherings are excellent opportunities to learn from experienced foragers and to share your experiences.

# Tools and Techniques for Effective Foraging

The right tools can make a substantial difference in your foraging success. A good foraging knife, a basket or mesh bag, and a field guide are essential items. In the Southeast, a small shovel can also be useful for digging up tubers, like wild onions or Jerusalem artichokes.

## Safety First: Knowing What's Safe to Eat

One of the most important aspects of foraging is ensuring what you harvest is safe to eat.[80]

One of the most important aspects of foraging is ensuring what you harvest is safe to eat. Some plants have toxic look-alikes, so accurate identification is crucial. For instance, wild carrots (Queen Anne's lace) have a toxic look-alike called poison hemlock, which is deadly. Learning to differentiate between them is essential.

Always double-check your identifications with multiple sources before consuming wild plants. Consult experienced foragers or use identification apps like PlantSnap or iNaturalist when in doubt.

### Continuing the Foraging Journey

Foraging is not a one-time adventure but a continuous journey of discovery and learning. You should continue to find opportunities for further exploration to fully embrace a foraging lifestyle. Whether through educational events, joining local groups, or spending more time outdoors, there are many ways to keep your foraging journey alive and thriving.

### Opportunities for Further Exploration

One of the best ways to expand your foraging knowledge is by attending workshops and educational events. These gatherings offer a chance to learn from experienced foragers, botanists, and naturalists. For example, in the Southeast, you may find workshops on identifying edible mushrooms in the Appalachian Mountains or guided foraging tours in the Everglades.

Keep an eye on local nature centers, botanical gardens, and environmental organizations for upcoming events. Institutions like the Atlanta Botanical Garden or the North Carolina Arboretum often host foraging workshops and nature walks. These events provide hands-on learning experiences and connect with experts in the field.

### Joining Local Foraging Groups

Joining a foraging group can be a great way to meet like-minded individuals and learn from others' experiences. These groups often organize group foraging outings, share tips and recipes, and provide a supportive community for novice and experienced foragers. In the Southeast, groups are dedicated to specific interests, such as mushroom hunting or wild herbalism. Look for local foraging groups on social media platforms like Facebook or Meetup.

### Spending More Time in Nature

Make it a habit to spend more time outdoors to truly connect with the natural world. Regularly immersing yourself in nature improves your foraging skills and enhances your overall well-being. Explore various habitats and observe the seasonal changes in your local environment.

Plan weekly or monthly nature outings, whether a hike in a nearby state park, a stroll along a riverbank, or a visit to a local nature reserve. Bring a field guide and spend time identifying plants and fungi. The more familiar you become with your local ecosystem, the more successful and rewarding your foraging trips will be.

### Sharing Your Knowledge and Experiences

Sharing your knowledge and experiences with others can be incredibly rewarding as you continue your foraging journey. Teaching friends and family about foraging spreads awareness and reinforces your learning. You might just inspire others to start their own foraging adventures.

Host a foraging walk or a wild food dinner for your friends and family. Share what you've learned about identifying and preparing wild foods. You could consider starting a blog or social media page to document your foraging experiences and share tips and recipes with a broader audience.

### Integrating Foraged Foods into Everyday Life

Foraging isn't only about the adventure of finding wild foods. It's about incorporating them into your daily life. Integrating foraged foods can add richness and variety to your diet, from cooking and preserving to experimenting with new flavors.

### Incorporating Wild Ingredients into Daily Meals

One of the simplest ways to use foraged foods is by incorporating them into your everyday meals. Many wild edibles can easily be added to everyday dishes. For example, wild greens like dandelion, purslane, and chickweed are abundant in the Southeast and can be used like spinach or kale.

Try adding chopped chickweed to your morning omelet or mixing purslane into your lunchtime salad. Dandelion greens can be sautéed with garlic and olive oil as a side dish or blended into a smoothie for a nutrient boost. These small changes can make your meals more exciting and healthy.

### Creative Cooking with Foraged Foods

Foraged foods offer unique flavors that inspire creativity in the kitchen. Experimenting with these ingredients can result in delicious and unexpected culinary creations. Consider the diverse range of wild berries, nuts, and mushrooms available in the Southeast, such as blackberries, hickory nuts, and chanterelles.

Use wild berries to make homemade jams, jellies, or desserts like pies and cobblers. Hickory nuts can be roasted and added to granola or used in baking. Chanterelle mushrooms are excellent in risotto, pasta dishes, or sautéed with butter and herbs. Don't be afraid to experiment and discover new favorite recipes.

### Preserving Seasonal Harvests

Preserving foraged foods allows you to enjoy the flavors of each season long after the harvest. Techniques like drying, freezing, pickling, and making preserves extend the shelf life of wild foods and ensure you have a steady supply throughout the year.

Dry herbs like mint, nettle, and wild oregano to create herbal teas. Freeze berries and mushrooms for smoothies, sauces, and soups; pickle wild greens - such as ramps or fiddlehead ferns - to add tangy flavors to your meals. Making preserves, like elderberry syrup or sumac lemonade concentrate, can capture the essence of summer for the colder months.

### Exploring New Flavors and Culinary Techniques

Foraged foods often have unique and intense flavors that can transform ordinary dishes. Exploring these new tastes can be fun and rewarding. For example, the Southeast is home to the pawpaw, some fruit with a flavor reminiscent of banana and mango, and the spicebush, whose berries and leaves can be used as a seasoning.

Make a pawpaw pudding or ice cream to enjoy its tropical flavor. Use spicebush berries as a substitute for allspice in your recipes, or steep the leaves to make a fragrant tea. Incorporating these unique ingredients can elevate your cooking and introduce you to new culinary traditions.

### Preserving Nutritional Value

When integrating foraged foods into your diet, preserving their nutritional value is important. Many wild edibles are highly nutritious, but improper preparation can reduce their benefits. For example, some greens should be blanched before freezing to preserve their vitamins, and certain mushrooms need thorough cooking to remove toxins.

Research the best methods for preparing and preserving each foraged food. For instance, blanch dandelion greens before freezing them to maintain their color and nutrients. Cook mushrooms like morels and chanterelles thoroughly to ensure they are safe to eat and to enhance their flavors.

### Sharing Foraged Meals with Others

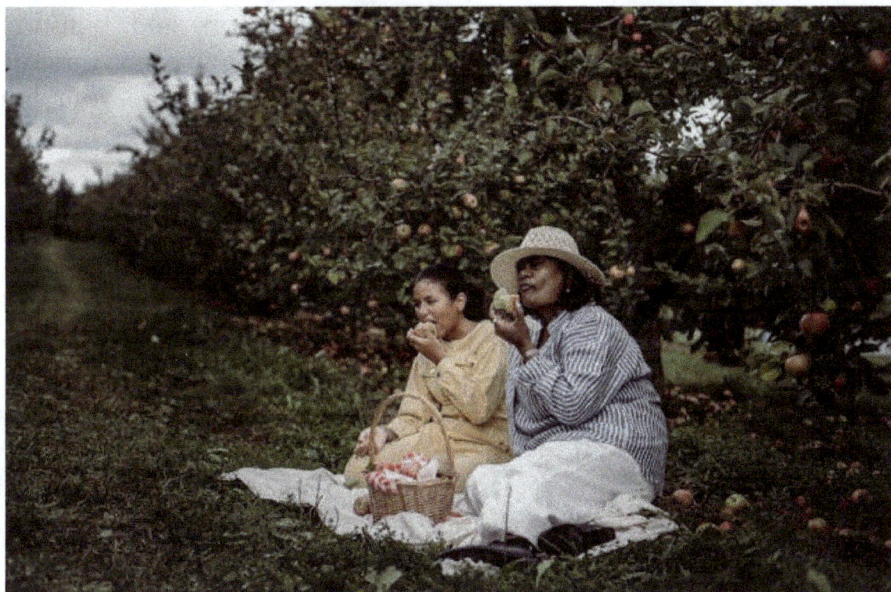

One of the joys of foraging is sharing your harvest and culinary creations with others.[51]

One of the joys of foraging is sharing your harvest and culinary creations with others. Hosting a meal featuring foraged foods can introduce friends and family to the delights of wild eating and inspire them to join you on your foraging adventures.

Plan a wild food dinner party and create a menu showcasing your foraged ingredients. Start with a salad of wild greens and edible flowers, follow with a main course featuring wild mushrooms or game, and finish with a dessert made from foraged berries. Sharing these meals can create memorable experiences and foster a sense of community.

### Keeping Safety in Mind

While foraging can be a rewarding and delicious endeavor, safety is paramount. Correctly identifying plants and fungi is crucial, as many have toxic look-alikes. Always be 100% certain of your identification before consuming wild food.

Apps like PlantSnap and iNaturalist will help with identification. However, always cross-reference with a reliable source. When in doubt, consult experienced foragers or local experts.

# Preserving and Storing Foraged Foods

Preserving and storing foraged foods is essential to making the most of your wild harvests. Proper techniques not only extend the shelf life of these seasonal treasures but also retain their flavors and nutritional benefits. In the Southeast, where diverse climates allow for a variety of edible plants and fungi, knowing how to preserve and store your finds effectively ensures you enjoy them year-round.

# Drying: A Simple and Effective Method

Drying is one of the oldest and simplest methods of preserving food. It works well for herbs, mushrooms, fruits, and some vegetables. Drying removes moisture, which inhibits the growth of bacteria, yeast, and mold.

Use a dehydrator for consistent results, or dry your harvests using natural sunlight or an oven set to a low temperature. For example, you can dry wild mushrooms like morels or chanterelles by slicing them thinly and placing them in a dehydrator. Dried mushrooms can be rehydrated in water for soups, stews, or sauces. Similarly, you can dry herbs, such as mint, thyme, and oregano, by hanging them in small bunches in a well-ventilated area away from direct sunlight.

### Freezing: Locking in Freshness

Freezing is ideal for preserving many foraged foods' freshness and nutritional value. It's particularly useful for berries, nuts, and some greens.

Wash and thoroughly dry your foraged foods before freezing. You can spread berries, like blackberries, elderberries, and mulberries, on a baking sheet to dry individually before transferring them to airtight containers or freezer bags. For greens like dandelion or chickweed, blanch them briefly in boiling water, then plunge them into ice water before freezing. This process preserves their color, texture, and nutrients.

### Pickling: Adding Zest to Your Pantry

Pickling is an excellent way to add flavor and preserve your foraged foods. It involves immersing them in a solution of vinegar, water, salt, and sometimes sugar and spices.

Pickle ramps, fiddlehead ferns, or wild garlic, as these will produce a tangy addition to salads, sandwiches, or charcuterie boards. Use a simple pickling brine of equal parts water and vinegar, with added salt and sugar to taste. Pack your cleaned and trimmed foraged vegetables into sterilized jars, pour the hot brine over them, and seal the jars. Let them sit in the refrigerator for at least a week before enjoying.

### Making Preserves: Sweet and Savory Spreads

Turning foraged fruits into jams, jellies, and preserves can capture the season's essence and provide delicious spreads for months.

Make wild berry jam using blackberries, elderberries, or muscadine grapes. Combine the cleaned fruit with sugar and a splash of lemon juice, then cook until thickened. Use pectin to help set the jam if desired. Pour the hot mixture into sterilized jars, seal, and process in a water bath canner for long-term storage.

### Fermenting: Beneficial Probiotics

Fermentation is a traditional preservation method that extends the food's shelf life and adds beneficial probiotics to your diet. It's excellent for wild vegetables and greens.

Ferment wild greens like lamb's quarters or purslane by mixing them with salt and packing them tightly into a jar. Use a fermentation weight to submerge the vegetables in their juices, and cover the jar with a breathable cloth. Let it ferment at room temperature for a week or more, periodically tasting until you achieve the desired flavor. Fermented greens can be used like sauerkraut or kimchi.

### Making Tinctures: Preserving Medicinal Herbs

Tinctures are a way to preserve the medicinal properties of herbs using alcohol or glycerin. They are particularly useful for herbs like wild mint, yarrow, and elderflower.

To make a tincture, chop fresh or dried herbs and place them in a jar. Cover the herbs with alcohol (such as vodka), or alternatively, use glycerin. Seal the jar and let it sit in a dark place for several weeks, shaking occasionally. Strain the mixture through a fine mesh sieve or cheesecloth and store the tincture in dark glass bottles. Use tinctures in small doses as herbal remedies.

### Root Cellaring: Traditional Storage

Root cellaring is an age-old method of storing hardy vegetables and fruits in a cool, dark, and humid environment. It's perfect for root vegetables and late-season harvests.

Store root vegetables like wild carrots, Jerusalem artichokes, and burdock roots in a root cellar or a cool, dark basement. Layer them in boxes filled with sand or sawdust to maintain humidity and prevent them from drying out. Check regularly for signs of spoilage and remove affected items to preserve the rest.

### Vacuum Sealing: Modern Preservation

Vacuum sealing removes air from storage bags or containers, preventing oxidation and extending the shelf life of your foraged foods.

Use a vacuum sealer to store dried mushrooms, nuts, or freeze-dried berries. Place the food in vacuum seal bags, remove the air using the vacuum sealer, and store it in a cool, dark place. Vacuum-sealed foods can last significantly longer than those stored in regular containers.

## Practical Tips for Effective Storage

- **Labeling:** Always label your preserved foods with the item's name and the date it was preserved. It helps you keep track of freshness and use older items first.

- **Storage Conditions:** Store preserved foods in a cool, dark, dry place to maximize shelf life. Avoid exposure to direct sunlight and temperature fluctuations.

- **Rotation:** Practice first-in, first-out (FIFO) rotation in your pantry. Use the oldest preserved items first to ensure nothing goes to waste.

Living a foraging lifestyle in the Southeast is more than merely a way to find food. It's a holistic approach to life, fostering a deep connection with nature, promoting sustainability, and enhancing well-being. Ultimately, living a foraging lifestyle is about finding meaning and purpose in your relationship with Earth. It's about recognizing your place in the natural world. Foraging teaches you to slow down, observe, and appreciate the simple joys of nature. It reminds you of your interconnectedness and responsibility to protect and cherish the environment.

# Bonus: Southeast Foraging Calendar

## Southeast Foraging Calendar

❄ Winter  🌱 Spring  ☀ Summer  🍂 Fall

| | Jan | Feb | Mar | Apr | May | Jun | Jul | Aug | Sep | Oct | Nov | Dec |
|---|---|---|---|---|---|---|---|---|---|---|---|---|
| **SPRING** | | | | | | | | | | | | |
| Acer spp. (Maple) | | | ■ | 🌱 | | | | | | | | |
| Urtica dioica (stinging nettle) | | | ■ | 🌱 | | | | | | | | |
| Plantago spp. (plantain) | | | ■ | ■ | 🌱 | | | | | | | |
| Acorus calamus (Calamus, sweet flag) | | | | ■ | ■ | ■ | ■ | 🌱 | | | | |
| Viola spp. (violet) | | | ■ | 🌱 | | | | | | | | |
| Celtis occidentalis (hackberry) | | | ■ | ■ | 🌱 | | | | | | | |
| Amaranthus spp. (amaranth, pigweed) | | | | | ■ | 🌱 | | | | | | |
| Daucus carota (wild carrot) | | | | | ■ | ■ | ■ | ■ | 🌱 | | | |
| Rorippa nasturtium aquaticum (watercress) | | | | | ■ | ■ | ■ | ■ | 🌱 | | | |
| Asarum spp. (wild ginger) | | | | | ■ | ■ | ■ | ■ | 🌱 | | | |
| Stellaria media (chickweed) | | | | ■ | ■ | ■ | ■ | 🌱 | | | | |
| Typha spp. (cattail) | | | | | ■ | ■ | ■ | ■ | 🌱 | | | |

| | Winter | Spring | Summer | Fall | Jan | Feb | Mar | Apr | May | Jun | Jul | Aug | Sep | Oct | Nov | Dec |
|---|---|---|---|---|---|---|---|---|---|---|---|---|---|---|---|---|

## SUMMER

| | Jan | Feb | Mar | Apr | May | Jun | Jul | Aug | Sep | Oct | Nov | Dec |
|---|---|---|---|---|---|---|---|---|---|---|---|---|
| Rhus spp. (sumac) | | | | | | ■ | ■ | ☀ | | | | |
| Sambucus canadensis (common elder, elderberry) | | | | | ■ | ■ | ☀ | | | | | |
| Chenopodium spp. (lamb's-quarters) | | | | | ■ | ■ | ■ | ■ | ☀ | | | |
| Ribes spp. (currant, gooseberry) | | | | | | ■ | ■ | ■ | ☀ | | | |

## FALL

| | Jan | Feb | Mar | Apr | May | Jun | Jul | Aug | Sep | Oct | Nov | Dec |
|---|---|---|---|---|---|---|---|---|---|---|---|---|
| Asimina triloba (pawpaw) | | | | | | | | | ☘ | | | |
| Physalis spp. (ground cherry) | | | | | | | | | ☘ | | | |
| Sagittaria spp. (Arrowhead, wapatoo) | | | | | | | | | | ☘ | | |
| Triosteum spp. (tinker's weed, wild coffee, horse gentian) | | | | | | | | | ■ | ☘ | | |

## WINTER

| | Jan | Feb | Mar | Apr | May | Jun | Jul | Aug | Sep | Oct | Nov | Dec |
|---|---|---|---|---|---|---|---|---|---|---|---|---|
| Carya spp. (hickory) | | | | | | | | | | ■ | ■ | ❄ |
| Gaultheria procumbens (wintergreen) | | | | | | | | | ■ | ■ | ■ | ❄ |
| Barbarea verna, B. vulgaris (wintercress) | ■ | ❄ | | | | | | | | | | ❄ |
| Sonchus spp. (sow thistle roots) | | | | | | | | | | | ■ | ❄ |

# Index: A-Z of Wild Edibles, Mushrooms, and Medicinal Plants

This chapter enlists wild edible plants and fungi commonly found in the Southeast region.

## Wild Edible Index

# Conclusion

Now that you've reached the end of this book, you're ready to put the knowledge you've gained into practice. Hopefully, this book has reinforced your passion and interest in foraging and given you the confidence to head outside and examine the local plants in your area. Foraging is much more than a pastime. It's a holistic lifestyle to help boost mental, emotional, and physical health. Spending time in a natural environment and examining its ecosystem can help alleviate stress and anxiety. It's an opportunity to unwind from the stressors of daily life and learn to be present in the moment.

Foraging is a great mindfulness practice that helps you regulate your emotions, boost focus, and encourage you to become attuned to your thoughts, feelings, physical sensations, and surroundings. Foraging lets you stay active and enriches your diet, boosting your overall well-being.

Reading this book, you've explored the rich, diverse landscape of the Southeastern region of the United States. You understand how to differentiate between poisonous, edible, and inedible mushrooms and fungi and to recognize wild edible and medicinal plants. You gained insight into the seasonal foraging patterns and practices and understood how to forage safely and ethically.

The culinary landscape of foraged plants is one of the most exciting aspects of the practice. In Chapter 6, you discovered delicious dishes using wild edibles and how to incorporate them into your diet. Moreover, you explored the various ways you can harness medicinal plants' healing powers, and the book explained how to integrate them into your holistic wellness routine.

Cultivating a foraging mindset will help you maintain a sustainable lifestyle. Harvesting wild plants encourages people to use naturally grown, local resources, benefitting the environment when done ethically and safely. Foraging reduces carbon footprint, as it doesn't require using transportation, reducing the emission of greenhouse gases. It promotes biodiversity, as many foragers advocate for the preservation of natural ecosystems and habitats. Foraging minimizes the impact of harmful agricultural tools on the environment. Those who forage only take what they need from the environment, eliminating overconsumption and ensuring enough plants are left to regenerate.

Foraging is a sustainable practice that not only benefits the environment but also boosts your mental, physical, and emotional health. It allows you to establish a deep relationship with nature and changes your perspective about life. Use the tips, knowledge, and information you gained reading this book, and embrace the benefits of foraging.

If you enjoyed this book, I'd greatly appreciate a review on Amazon because it helps me to create more books that people want. It would mean a lot to hear from you.

**To leave a review:**

1. Open your camera app.
2. Point your mobile device at the QR code.
3. The review page will appear in your web browser.

---

*Thanks for your support!*

# Here's another book by Dion Rosser that you might like

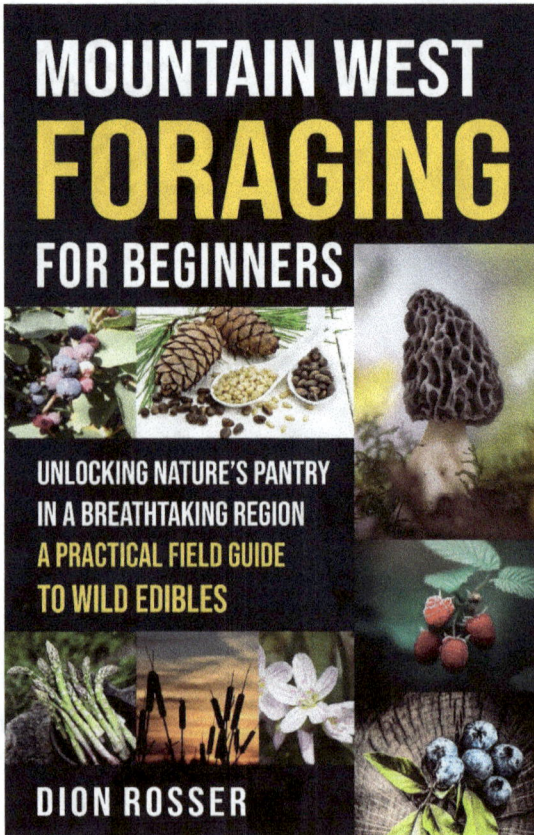

MOUNTAIN WEST
FORAGING
FOR BEGINNERS

UNLOCKING NATURE'S PANTRY
IN A BREATHTAKING REGION
A PRACTICAL FIELD GUIDE
TO WILD EDIBLES

DION ROSSER

# References

A Guide to Foraging in Alabama and the Southeast – Feral Foraging. (2023, November 21). https://feralforaging.com/foraging-alabama-and-southeast/

Alabama Mushroom Society – Common Edible Mushrooms. (n.d.). Alabamamushroomsociety.org. https://alabamamushroomsociety.org/common-edible-mushrooms

An Introduction to Edible Plants in the Southeast – The... (2016, December 5). https://thesurvivalsummit.com/2016-12-5-an-introduction-to-edible-plants-in-the-southeast/

Baillargeon, Z. (2021, August 17). Want to Be an Ethical, Sustainable Forager? Here's Your Guide. Field Mag. https://www.fieldmag.com/articles/sustainable-ethical-foraging-guide

Bergo, A. (2018, June 15). Wood Nettles. Forager Chef. https://foragerchef.com/wood-nettles-laportea-canadensis/

Blankespoor, J., & Gemma, M. (2019, March 8). Essential Foraging Tools and Supplies. Chestnut School of Herbal Medicine. https://chestnutherbs.com/essential-foraging-tools-and-supplies/

Bottino, B. (2022, June 26). Poisonous plants and venomous animals hazards for outdoor workers | Safety+Health. Www.safetyandhealthmagazine.com. https://www.safetyandhealthmagazine.com/articles/22739-poisonous-plants-venomous-animals-outdoor-workers?page=2

Chef Dhuha. (2024). Sumac Salad. Www.cuisineathome.com. https://www.cuisineathome.com/recipes/side-dishes/sumac-salad/

Chelsweets. (2021, May 13). Blackberry Overnight Oats – The Perfect Make-Ahead Breakfast. Chelsweets. https://chelsweets.com/blackberry-overnight-oats/

Colleen Codekas. (2019, April 3). Grow Forage Cook Ferment. https://www.growforagecookferment.com/what-to-forage-in-spring/

College of Arts and Sciences. (n.d.). Seasonal Schedule of Edible Wild Plants in Southeastern Ohio | Ohio University. Www.ohio.edu. https://www.ohio.edu/cas/plant-biology/research/facilities-laboratories/edible-wild-plants-se-ohio/seasonal

Eat The Weeds and other things, too. (n.d.). Eat the Weeds and Other Things, Too. https://www.eattheweeds.com/

Edible Wild Food, Recipes | Weeds, Fungi, Flowers & Foraging. (2019). Ediblewildfood.com. https://www.ediblewildfood.com/

Evergreen Garden Care. (n.d.). How to maintain and care for your gardening tools. Love the Garden. https://www.lovethegarden.com/uk-en/article/how-maintain-and-care-your-gardening-tools

Ferment, G. F. C. (2024, April 18). Dandelion Salad: A Recipe from Grandma's Time. Grow Forage Cook Ferment. https://www.growforagecookferment.com/dandelion-salad/#recipe

Flowers, J. (2021, April 15). Fried Chicken of the Woods Sandwich. Wild Vegan Flower. https://wildveganflower.com/fried-chicken-of-the-woods-sandwich/#wprm-recipe-container-30348

Foraging Alaska: The Quest For Sustainable Foods. (n.d.). Foraged & Found. https://foragednfound.com/pages/wild-harvested-foraged-foods

Foraging for Wild Edibles and Herbs: Sustainable and Safe Gathering Practices. (2017, November 7). Chestnut School of Herbal Medicine. https://chestnutherbs.com/foraging-for-wild-edibles-and-herbs-sustainable-and-safe-gathering-practices/

Foraging in Early Spring: Wild Edible Plants to Gather Now. (n.d.). Good Life Revival. https://thegoodliferevival.com/blog/foraging-spring-wild-edible-plants

Gibson, A. (2018, February 9). Build a Toolkit for Spring Foraging. Mount Baker Experience. https://www.mountbakerexperience.com/stories/build-a-toolkit-for-spring-foraging,559

Graham, C. (2022, June 6). Foraging: Inside the Modern Resurgence of an Ancient Art. Sustainableamerica.org. https://sustainableamerica.org/blog/foraging-inside-the-modern-resurgence-of-ancient-art

Grant, C. (2022, May 12). Black Locust Flower Jelly. Unruly Gardening. https://unrulygardening.com/black-locust-flower-jelly/

greenlivingguy. (2021, December 13). What You Need to Know About Foraging and Its Impact on the Earth. Green Living Guy. https://greenlivingguy.com/2021/12/what-you-need-to-know-about-foraging-and-its-impact-on-the-earth

Harvard Health. (2019, March 21). Benefits of Mindfulness – HelpGuide.org. https://www.helpguide.org/harvard/benefits-of-mindfulness.htm.

Hay, M. E. (2020, July 9). Interest in Foraging Is Booming. Here's How to Do it Right. Civil Eats. https://civileats.com/2020/07/09/interest-in-foraging-is-booming-heres-how-to-do-it-right/

Hayes, J. (2022, March 4). How to start foraging and what equipment you will need when out and about. The Secret Garden. https://the-secret-garden.net/how-to-start-foraging-and-what-you-will-need-when-out-and-about.html

Henofthewood. (2016, March 1). The Foraged Foodie: Foraging: What is in Season, Early Spring. The Foraged Foodie. https://foragedfoodie.blogspot.com/2016/03/Foragingearlyspring.html

Hudson, A. (2024, March 31). Ethical Considerations for Foraging Wild Plants. Book Wild Food Foraging Classes Online | ForageSF. https://www.foragesf.com/blog/ethical-considerations-for-foraging-wild-plants

International Culinary Center. (2018, November 28). How to Safely Forage | Institute of Culinary Education. Www.ice.edu. https://www.ice.edu/blog/how-to-safely-forage

Jenny. (2024, March 7). Spring Mushroom Foraging In The Southeast – Mushroom Appreciation. Www.mushroom-Appreciation.com. https://www.mushroom-appreciation.com/spring-mushroom-southeast.html

Joanna. (2020, January 17). Jerusalem Artichoke Soup – taste botanical – very easy vegetarian recipe. Tastebotanical. https://tastebotanical.com/jerusalem-artichoke-soup/

Kemp, J. (2010, December 29). Vegan chickweed pesto – Juliet Kemp. Julietkemp.com. https://julietkemp.com/2010/12/vegan-chickweed-pesto/

Kravchuk, N. (2015, November 4). Persimmon Bread Recipe. NatashasKitchen.com. https://natashaskitchen.com/persimmon-bread-recipe/

Krochmal, A., Walters, R., Doughty, R., & Service, U. (n.d.). A Guide to MEDICINAL PLANTS. https://www.fs.usda.gov/nrs/pubs/rp/rp_ne138.pdf

MacKinnon, K., & Wiles, B. (2020, September 17). The beginner's guide to foraging. Backpacker. https://www.backpacker.com/skills/foraging/

Macri, I. (2023, September 25). Pecan-Crusted Chicken With Honey & Garlic. Cooked & Loved. https://www.cookedandloved.com/recipes/pecan-crusted-chicken/#recipe

Mihail, A. (2023, July 11). Foraging in The Modern World: Rediscovering an Ancient Practice. Www.foodunfolded.com. https://www.foodunfolded.com/article/foraging-in-the-modern-world-rediscovering-an-ancient-practice

Mushroom Foraging Seasons of the Southeast – Feral Foraging. (2021, February 4). https://feralforaging.com/mushroom-foraging-seasons-of-the-southeast/

Oijala, L. (2013, January 28). Make Your Own Lung-Healing Herbal Tea with Mullein – Organic Authority. Www.organicauthority.com. https://www.organicauthority.com/health/mullein-herbal-tea/

Red Clover herb uses Trifolium pratense. (n.d.). Altnature.com. https://altnature.com/gallery/redclover.htm

Shane, C. (2023, November 16). Herbs of the Coastal Plain. Blue Ridge School of Herbal Medicine. https://blueridgeschool.org/herbs-of-the-coastal-plain/

Shaw, H. (2012, June 19). Elderflower Fritters Recipe – How to Make Elderflower Fritters. Hunter Angler Gardener Cook. https://honest-food.net/elderflower-fritter-recipe/

Shaw, H. (2024, June 3). Elderflower Syrup Recipe – How to Make Elderflower Cordial. Hunter Angler Gardener Cook. https://honest-food.net/elderflower-cordial/#wprm-recipe-container-23921

Slow Living Kitchen. (2023, June 26). 10 Tips for Cooking with Wild Edibles. YouTube. https://www.youtube.com/watch?v=L9tQPaJ1-yY

Staff Writer. (2022, May 9). Poisonous Mushrooms to Avoid When Foraging. The Habitat. https://thehabitat.com/garden/poisonous-mushrooms-to-avoid-when-foraging/7/

Stalking the South's Wild Edibles. (n.d.). THE BITTER SOUTHERNER. https://bittersoutherner.com/foraging-the-south-pfitzer-hosey-forson

Tennessee Agricultural Extension Service. (1980). Poisonous Plants of the Southeastern United States. https://giles.tennessee.edu/wp-content/uploads/sites/194/2020/10/Ag-Poisonous-Plants-of-the-Southeastern-United-States.pdf

The history of gathering food | alimentarium. (n.d.). Www.alimentarium.org. https://www.alimentarium.org/en/fact-sheet/history-gathering-food

Trust, W. (n.d.-a). Foraging Guide – Month by Month. Woodland Trust. https://www.woodlandtrust.org.uk/visiting-woods/things-to-do/foraging/

Trust, W. (n.d.-b). Foraging in March: spring's edible plants. Woodland Trust. https://www.woodlandtrust.org.uk/blog/2018/03/foraging-in-march/

Twitter, & University, F. (n.d.). Identifying Wild Mushrooms: A Guide to Edible and Poisonous Mushrooms. Treehugger. https://www.treehugger.com/wild-mushrooms-what-to-eat-what-to-avoid-4864324

Types of Edible Wild Mushrooms Archives. (n.d.). FORAGER | CHEF. https://foragerchef.com/category/wild-mushroom-species/

Unpeeled. (2023, February 21). Wild Mushroom Risotto. Unpeeled Journal. https://unpeeledjournal.com/mushroom-risotto-recipe/

Wild Edibles & Medicinal Plants. (n.d.). Georgia Bushcraft. https://www.georgiabushcraft.com/blogs/wild-edibles-medicinal-plants

Winter Mushroom Foraging In The Southeast – Mushroom Appreciation. (2023, December 18). Www.mushroom-Appreciation.com. https://www.mushroom-appreciation.com/winter-mushroom-foraging-in-the-southeast.html

wonderlicious. (2024, January 18). Here Are The Highly Recommended Spring Foraging Experiences That Nordic Countries Love. Wonderlicious. https://wonderlicious.blog/2024/01/18/here-are-the-highly-recommended-spring-foraging-experiences-that-nordic-countries-offer/

Yarrow, Achillea millefolium, Herb Use and Pictures. (n.d.). Altnature.com. https://altnature.com/gallery/yarrow.htm

# Image Sources

[1] *Witte Museum, CC BY-SA 4.0 <https://creativecommons.org/licenses/by-sa/4.0>, via Wikimedia Commons: https://commons.wikimedia.org/wiki/File:Food_Gathering_Diorama_from_People_of_the_Pecos_Gallery.jpg*

[2] *https://www.pexels.com/photo/person-holding-allergy-medicine-bottle-6865181/*

[3] *https://www.pexels.com/photo/trees-and-grass-field-under-cloudy-sky-during-daytime-186980/*

[4] *Gmihail at Serbian Wikipedia, CC BY-SA 3.0 RS <https://creativecommons.org/licenses/by-sa/3.0/rs/deed.en>, via Wikimedia Commons: https://commons.wikimedia.org/wiki/File:Bypass_pruners_and_hardwood_cuttings.jpg*

[5] *Santeri Viinamäki, CC BY-SA 4.0 <https://creativecommons.org/licenses/by-sa/4.0>, via Wikimedia Commons: https://commons.wikimedia.org/wiki/File:Shovel_leaning_against_a_wall.jpg*

[6] *Doggerelblogger, CC BY-SA 4.0 <https://creativecommons.org/licenses/by-sa/4.0>, via Wikimedia Commons: https://commons.wikimedia.org/wiki/File:Kitchen_scissors.jpg*

[7] *Santeri Viinamäki, CC BY-SA 4.0 <https://creativecommons.org/licenses/by-sa/4.0>, via Wikimedia Commons: https://commons.wikimedia.org/wiki/File:Blue_pitchfork.jpg*

[8] *https://www.pexels.com/photo/damascus-steel-knives-on-a-black-background-kitchen-knives-background-with-japanese-knife-a-set-of-japanese-damascus-steel-knives-banner-16603814/*

[9] *Simon A. Eugster, CC BY-SA 3.0 <https://creativecommons.org/licenses/by-sa/3.0>, via Wikimedia Commons: https://commons.wikimedia.org/wiki/File:Asts%C3%A4ge.jpg*

[10] *https://www.pexels.com/photo/dish-brush-set-and-soap-10573239/*

[11] *https://pexels.com/photo/person-wearing-a-tool-belt-8447885/*

[12] *https://www.pexels.com/photo/green-leaves-on-top-of-open-book-near-paint-brush-and-green-snake-plant-on-pot-2099266/*

[13] https://www.pexels.com/photo/a-woman-wearing-garden-gloves-touching-the-leaves-of-strawberry-plant-7457195/

[14] https://www.pexels.com/photo/tilt-shift-lens-photography-of-person-holding-magnifying-glass-1192333/

[15] https://www.pexels.com/photo/woman-in-red-tank-top-and-white-shorts-carrying-backpack-sitting-on-brown-grass-field-3756035/

[16] https://www.pexels.com/photo/three-clear-glass-jars-on-gray-surface-1640767/

[17] https://www.pexels.com/photo/stacked-brown-wicker-baskets-94296/

[18] SEWilco, CC BY-SA 3.0 <https://creativecommons.org/licenses/by-sa/3.0>, via Wikimedia Commons: https://commons.wikimedia.org/wiki/File:Five_gallon_bucket_20080716.jpg

[19] Knowledge at Dutch Wikipedia, CC BY-SA 3.0 <http://creativecommons.org/licenses/by-sa/3.0/>, via Wikimedia Commons: https://commons.wikimedia.org/wiki/File:Walkie-talkie.JPG

[20] https://www.pexels.com/photo/overhead-shot-of-a-compass-near-flowers-7235813/

[21] https://www.pexels.com/photo/first-aid-kit-on-gray-background-5673523/

[22] Reem Al-Kashif, CC BY-SA 4.0 <https://creativecommons.org/licenses/by-sa/4.0>, via Wikimedia Commons: https://commons.wikimedia.org/wiki/File:Food_in_Award_Ceremony_for_Winners_in_Wiki_Science_Photo_Competition_Egypt.jpg

[23] https://www.pexels.com/photo/yellow-flower-field-under-blue-cloudy-sky-during-daytime-46164/

[24] https://www.pexels.com/photo/three-assorted-color-pineapples-on-sand-137067/

[25] https://www.pexels.com/photo/brown-pistachio-nut-lot-634650/

[26] https://www.pexels.com/photo/photo-of-a-forest-in-winter-24589232/

[27] H. Zell, CC BY-SA 3.0 <https://creativecommons.org/licenses/by-sa/3.0>, via Wikimedia Commons: https://commons.wikimedia.org/wiki/File:Taraxacum_officinale_001.JPG

[28] Hugo.arg, CC BY-SA 4.0 <https://creativecommons.org/licenses/by-sa/4.0>, via Wikimedia Commons: https://commons.wikimedia.org/wiki/File:ChenopodiumAlbum001.JPG

[29] Giancarlo Dessì (Posted by --gian_d 21:26, 15 November 2006 (UTC)), CC BY-SA 3.0 <http://creativecommons.org/licenses/by-sa/3.0/>, via Wikimedia Commons https://commons.wikimedia.org/wiki/File:Portulaca_oleracea_g1.jpg

[30] Jay Sturner from USA, CC BY 2.0 <https://creativecommons.org/licenses/by/2.0>, via Wikimedia Commons: https://commons.wikimedia.org/wiki/File:Field_or_Wild_Garlic_(Allium_vineale)_-_Flickr_-_Jay_Sturner_(2).jpg

[31] Lazaregagnidze, CC BY-SA 4.0 <https://creativecommons.org/licenses/by-sa/4.0>, via Wikimedia Commons: https://commons.wikimedia.org/wiki/File:Stellaria_media_Common_Chickweed_%E1%83%9F%E1%83%A3%E1%83%9C%E1%83%9F%E1%83%A0%E1%83%A3%E1%83%99%E1%83%98.JPG

[32] Ryan Hodnett, CC BY-SA 4.0 <https://creativecommons.org/licenses/by-sa/4.0>, via Wikimedia Commons https://commons.wikimedia.org/wiki/File:Common_Blue_Violet_%28Viola_sororia%29_-_Montreal%2C_Quebec_2019-05-12.jpg

[33] Fritzflohrreynolds, CC BY-SA 3.0 <https://creativecommons.org/licenses/by-sa/3.0>, via Wikimedia Commons: https://commons.wikimedia.org/wiki/File:Cercis_canadensis_-_Eastern_Redbud_2.jpg

[34] Kor!An (Андрей Корзун), CC BY-SA 3.0 <https://creativecommons.org/licenses/by-sa/3.0>, via Wikimedia Commons: https://commons.wikimedia.org/wiki/File:Lonicera_sp._blooming_04.JPG

[35] Charles T. Bryson, USDA Agricultural Research Service, Bugwood.org, CC BY-SA 3.0 <https://creativecommons.org/licenses/by-sa/3.0>, via Wikimedia Commons https://commons.wikimedia.org/wiki/File:Sambucus_nigra_ssp_canadensis_2100034.jpg

[36] Cbaile19, CC0, via Wikimedia Commons https://commons.wikimedia.org/wiki/File:Hemerocallis_fulva%2C_2023-06-20%2C_South_Side%2C_01.jpg

[37] This file is licensed under the Creative Commons Attribution-Share Alike 3.0 Unported license, Attribution-ShareAlike 3.0 Unported, CC BY-SA 3, <https://creativecommons.org/licenses/by-sa/3.0/deed.en> via Wikimedia Commons.https://commons.wikimedia.org/wiki/File:Vaccinium_corymbosum%2801%29.jpg

[38] H. Zell, CC BY-SA 3.0 <https://creativecommons.org/licenses/by-sa/3.0>, via Wikimedia Commons: https://commons.wikimedia.org/wiki/File:Rubus_fruticosus_003.JPG

[39] Edal Anton Lefterov, CC BY-SA 3.0 <https://creativecommons.org/licenses/by-sa/3.0>, via Wikimedia Commons: https://commons.wikimedia.org/wiki/File:Sambucus-berries.jpg

[40] Malcolm Manners from Lakeland, FL, USA, CC BY 2.0 <https://creativecommons.org/licenses/by/2.0>, via Wikimedia Commons: https://commons.wikimedia.org/wiki/File:Maypop,_Passiflora_incarnata_(50228602788).jpg

[41] Jerry A. Payne, USDA Agricultural Research Service, CC BY 3.0 US <https://creativecommons.org/licenses/by/3.0/us/deed.en>, via Wikimedia Commons: https://commons.wikimedia.org/wiki/File:Carya_illinoinensis_foliagenuts1.jpg

[42] Arnstein Rønning, CC BY-SA 3.0 <https://creativecommons.org/licenses/by-sa/3.0>, via Wikimedia Commons: https://commons.wikimedia.org/wiki/File:Quercus_robur_nut.jpg

[43] No machine-readable author provided. Abrahami assumed (based on copyright claims). CC BY-SA 2.5 <https://creativecommons.org/licenses/by-sa/2.5>, via Wikimedia Commons: https://commons.wikimedia.org/wiki/File:Hickory_nuts_6060.JPG

[44] Bonnie Dalzell(bdalzell@qis.net), CC BY-SA 4.0 <https://creativecommons.org/licenses/by-sa/4.0>, via Wikimedia Commons https://commons.wikimedia.org/wiki/File:AlleghenyChinquapin-IMG_2802.JPG

[45] Ryan Hodnett, CC BY-SA 4.0 <https://creativecommons.org/licenses/by-sa/4.0>, via Wikimedia Commons: https://commons.wikimedia.org/wiki/File:Eastern_Black_Walnut_(Juglans_nigra)_-_Kitchener,_Ontario_2019-07-28.jpg

[46] Don McCulley, CC BY-SA 4.0 <https://creativecommons.org/licenses/by-sa/4.0>, via Wikimedia Commons https://commons.wikimedia.org/wiki/File:Chinese_yam_-_air-potato_-_dioscorea_polystachya_IMG_8134.jpg

[47] *Dalgial, CC BY 3.0 <https://creativecommons.org/licenses/by/3.0>, via Wikimedia Commons https://commons.wikimedia.org/wiki/File:Helianthus_tuberosus_2.JPG*

[48] *Lazaregagnidze, CC BY-SA 3.0 <https://creativecommons.org/licenses/by-sa/3.0>, via Wikimedia Commons: https://commons.wikimedia.org/wiki/File:Arctium_lappa_Great_Burdock_%E1%83%9D%E1%83%A0%E1%83%9D%E1%83%95%E1%83%90%E1%83%9C%E1%83%93%E1%83%98_(2).JPG*

[49] *Geoff Gallice from Gainesville, FL, USA, CC BY 2.0 <https://creativecommons.org/licenses/by/2.0>, via Wikimedia Commons https://commons.wikimedia.org/wiki/File:Flickr_-_ggallice_-_Man-of-the-Earth.jpg*

[50] *Zhousun21, CC0, via Wikimedia Commons: https://commons.wikimedia.org/wiki/File:Parts_of_a_mushroom.jpg*

[51] *Andreas Kunze, CC BY-SA 3.0 <https://creativecommons.org/licenses/by-sa/3.0>, via Wikimedia Commons: https://commons.wikimedia.org/wiki/File:2007-07-14_Cantharellus_cibarius.jpg*

[52] *Andrew C, CC BY 2.0 <https://creativecommons.org/licenses/by/2.0>, via Wikimedia Commons: https://commons.wikimedia.org/wiki/File:True_Morel_(Morchella_sp.)_(17182800705).jpg*

[53] *Henk Monster, CC BY 3.0 <https://creativecommons.org/licenses/by/3.0>, via Wikimedia Commons: https://commons.wikimedia.org/wiki/File:Grifola_frondosa_(GB%3D_Hen_of_the_Woods,_D%3D_Klapperschwamm,_F%3D_Polypore_en_touffes,_NL%3D_Eikhaas),_white_spores_and_causes_whiterot,_at_Rozendaal_forest_-_panoramio.jpg*

[54] *gailhampshire, CC BY 2.0 <https://creativecommons.org/licenses/by/2.0>, via Wikimedia Commons: https://commons.wikimedia.org/wiki/File:Lion%27s_Mane_Fungi._Hericium_erinaceus.jpg*

[55] *Bigredwine1, CC BY-SA 4.0 <https://creativecommons.org/licenses/by-sa/4.0>, via Wikimedia Commons: https://commons.wikimedia.org/wiki/File:Coprinus_comatus,_the_shaggy_ink_cap,_lawyer%27s_wig,_or_shaggy_mane_mushroom.jpg*

[56] *Holger Krisp, CC BY 3.0 <https://creativecommons.org/licenses/by/3.0>, via Wikimedia Commons: https://commons.wikimedia.org/wiki/File:Black_trumpet_Craterellus_cornucopioides.jpg*

[57] *Björn S..., CC BY-SA 2.0 <https://creativecommons.org/licenses/by-sa/2.0>, via Wikimedia Commons: https://commons.wikimedia.org/wiki/File:Russula_sp._(37128971585).jpg*

[58] *This image was created by user Bill (boletebill) at Mushroom Observer, a source for mycological images. You can contact this user here.English | español | français | italiano | македонски | português | +/ , CC BY-SA 3.0 <https://creativecommons.org/licenses/by-sa/3.0>, via Wikimedia Commons: https://commons.wikimedia.org/wiki/File:2018-10-05_Tricholoma_magnivelare_(Peck)_Redhead_972957.jpg*

[59] *This image was created by user Dan Molter (shroomydan) at Mushroom Observer, a source for mycological images. You can contact this user here.English | español | français | italiano | македонски | português | +/ , CC BY-SA 3.0 <https://creativecommons.org/licenses/by-sa/3.0>, via Wikimedia Commons https://commons.wikimedia.org/wiki/File:Hypomyces_lactifluorum_169126.jpg*

[60] https://www.pexels.com/photo/handbag-with-fresh-assorted-vegetables-on-table-4020557/

[61] https://www.pexels.com/photo/vegetable-salad-on-white-ceramic-plate-beside-grey-stainless-steel-fork-1152237/

[62] https://www.pexels.com/photo/delicious-desserts-in-glass-jars-on-kitchen-towel-with-a-pair-of-spoons-5803169/

[63] Kolforn (Wikimedia), CC BY-SA 4.0 <https://creativecommons.org/licenses/by-sa/4.0>, via Wikimedia Commons: https://commons.wikimedia.org/wiki/File:-2019-12-22_Mushroom_Risotto_with_onion_and_herbs_finished_with_Parmesan_and_Mushroom,_Trimingham.JPG

[64] Jooojay, CC BY-SA 4.0 <https://creativecommons.org/licenses/by-sa/4.0>, via Wikimedia Commons: https://commons.wikimedia.org/wiki/File:Duarte%27s_Tavern_soup.jpg

[65] https://www.pexels.com/photo/close-up-of-a-dish-in-a-bowl-6880227/

[66] https://www.pexels.com/photo/sweet-jelly-desert-with-blueberries-and-flowers-6469637/

[67] https://www.pexels.com/photo/clear-glass-bowl-beside-yellow-flower-1638280/

[68] https://www.pexels.com/photo/close-up-photo-of-alternative-medicines-7526013/

[69] Emőke Dénes, CC BY-SA 4.0 <https://creativecommons.org/licenses/by-sa/4.0>, via Wikimedia Commons: https://commons.wikimedia.org/wiki/File:Asterales_-_Echinacea_purpurea_-_4.jpg

[70] James St. John, CC BY 2.0 <https://creativecommons.org/licenses/by/2.0>, via Wikimedia Commons: https://commons.wikimedia.org/wiki/File:Hydrastis_canadensis_(goldenseal)_(Flint_Ridge,_Ohio,_USA)_3_(26158948004).jpg

[71] H. Zell, CC BY-SA 3.0 <https://creativecommons.org/licenses/by-sa/3.0>, via Wikimedia Commons: https://commons.wikimedia.org/wiki/File:Actaea_racemosa_006.JPG

[72] I, SB Johnny, CC BY-SA 3.0 <http://creativecommons.org/licenses/by-sa/3.0/>, via Wikimedia Commons: https://commons.wikimedia.org/wiki/File:Eupatorium_perfoliatum_001.JPG

[73] Miguel Vieira from Walnut Creek, CA, USA, CC BY 2.0 <https://creativecommons.org/licenses/by/2.0>, via Wikimedia Commons: https://commons.wikimedia.org/wiki/File:Saw_palmetto_(Serenoa_repens)_in_Manatee_Springs_State_Park.jpg

[74] Petar Milošević, CC BY-SA 4.0 <https://creativecommons.org/licenses/by-sa/4.0>, via Wikimedia Commons: https://commons.wikimedia.org/wiki/File:Yarrow_(Achillea_millefolium).jpg

[75] No machine-readable author provided. Valérie75 assumed (based on copyright claims)., CC BY-SA 3.0 <http://creativecommons.org/licenses/by-sa/3.0/>, via Wikimedia Commons: https://commons.wikimedia.org/wiki/File:Baptisia_tinctoria_001.jpg

[76] Ragesoss, CC BY-SA 3.0 <https://creativecommons.org/licenses/by-sa/3.0>, via Wikimedia Commons: https://commons.wikimedia.org/wiki/File:Ripe,_ripening,_and_green_blackberries.jpg

[77] H. Zell, CC BY-SA 3.0 <https://creativecommons.org/licenses/by-sa/3.0>, via Wikimedia Commons: https://commons.wikimedia.org/wiki/File:Althaea_officinalis_002.JPG

[78] Fritzflohrreynolds, CC BY-SA 3.0 <https://creativecommons.org/licenses/by-sa/3.0>, via Wikimedia Commons: https://commons.wikimedia.org/wiki/File:Hamamelis_virginiana_-